CLASSIFICATION: POETRY

A CIP catalogue record for this book is available from
the British Library.

Printed and bound in Great Britain.

Paper used in the production of books published by
United Press comes only from sustainable forests.

This North West England edition

ISBN 1-84436-266-3

First published in Great Britain in 2005 by
United Press Ltd
Admail 3735
London
EC1B 1JB
Tel: 0870 240 6190
Fax: 0870 240 6191
ISBN for complete set of volumes
1-84436-268-X
All Rights Reserved

www.unitedpress.co.uk

Affectionately Yours

Foreword

Love truly makes the world go round. It is the essence of life.

But like life itself, love is impossible to express, explain or understand. It is something that we can only feel. And if you haven't felt it, you will never understand it.

Poets through the ages have struggled to pin down on paper the unique and individual intimacy which is the fabric of love. So many have got so near but can they ever make us feel exactly what they feel when they talk about love?

In this volume a group of poets has dared to aim for the impossible - to define love and express it so that the reader can feel it as purely as they do.

It is a pleasure for us to be able to bring this volume to your hands, in the hope that you can identify with some of the feelings expressed in it.

Peter Quinn, Editor

Contents

The poets who have contributed to this volume are listed below, along with the relevant page upon which their work can be found.

	Marylyn Blackshaw	93	Iris Tennant
65	Margaret Rose		Oliver Waterer
66	Carol Edith Hopgood	94	Irene Charlton
	Val J Chapman	95	Linda Zulaica
67	Sandra Mooney	96	Susan Entwistle
68	Rebecca Davis		Jeanette Hyde
	Sheila Ellis	97	Sheila M Borrowdale
69	Prakash Solanki	98	Grace Wallace
70	Jo Rainford	99	Constance M Price
	Hazel Wellings	100	Christopher Taylor
71	Colin Halsall		Dorothy Greenall
72	Alison Worsley	101	James Wright Ashcroft
	Rosaleen Dean	102	Karen Pickup
73	Jean Fogo	103	Magaret Fairhurst
74	Joan Salisbury	104	Tarni Procter
	Shirley C Daniels	105	Beryl Hall
75	Doris Thomson	106	Eric Dodgson
76	Adrian Johnson		Estelle Blackman
	Heather Ferrier	107	Elizabeth Saynor
77	Matthew Taylor	108	Monica Cole
	Vi Binns	109	Vera Entwistle
78	Lilian Hart	110	David Anderson
79	Graham Scotson	111	Jean Emmett
	Maureen Harrison	112	Rebekah Foulkes
	Riley	113	Clifford Chambers
80	Frances Rochelle	114	Eric Irwin
	Barrie	115	Rachel Butterworth
81	Alice J Campbell	116	Joseph Alston
	Sylvia Lee-Wild	117	Ben Lee Almond
82	Sheila Valerie Baldwin	118	Elsie Ryan
83	Pamela Igoe Hall	119	Winifred Smith
	Kelly Morgan		Emma-Jayne Toland
84	Stuart McEwen	120	Freda Grieve
85	Danny Milne	121	Marj Kurthausen
86	David Keevil		Janet Forster-Foote
87	Joan M Jones	122	Anthony Clements
	Ron Walls	123	Thomas McCabe
88	Dorothy M Ellis		Frances Brothers
89	Margaret Mohyla	124	Lynda Day-Bidston
90	Susan Atkinson	125	John Michael Corfe
	Geoffrey W Lever	126	David Lunn
91	Dawn Prestwich		Martha Birch
92	Ruth Zardecki	127	Joan Miller

	Janet Morris Evans	159	Clare Bell
128	Kathleen Baccino	160	Ann Christine
129	Ann Blair		Robertson
130	Catherine Chesters	161	Kathleen Evans
	Pat Fearon	162	Dawn Graham
131	Christine Hale	163	Geoff Hunter
132	Neville Davies	164	Tracey Turner
133	Albert Carpenter	165	Ruth Cooper
	Albert Pearson	166	May Foreman
134	Eve Ellen Williams		Julie Porter
135	Barbara Langton	167	John Patterson
	Tracy Costello	168	Iris Gibson
136	Monicah Downey	169	John Griffin
137	Kim-Marie Fisher	170	Marie Kay
138	Chris Terry		Dorothy A Harwood
	Hilary McShane	171	Barbara Jardine
139	Juliana Bond	172	Jim Haslam
140	Andrew Bruce	173	Jeremy Greenwood
	Celia Pope	174	Mabel Harrison
141	Janet Morris-Evans		Marion Kaye
142	Peter Price	175	Suzanne Jenkinson
143	Wendy Black	176	Gillian Sawyer
	Meleeze Zenda		Harriet Pomfret
144	Frankie Shepherd	177	Margery Mahon
145	Harry Boyle	178	Tony Cullen
146	Ruth Hayes	179	Pamela McNamara
	Philip Johnson	180	James Michael
147	Anna Connolly		Thomas
148	M R Armstrong		Helen Melrose
149	Paula Burke	181	Carmel Allison
150	Lorraine Thomas	182	Wendy Woodhead
151	Annette Smith	183	Jean Turner
	Susan Williams	184	John A Rickard
152	Danielle Mellor	185	Vikki Payne
153	Christina Shepherd		George Donnellan
	Jim Moss	186	Lil Bordessa
154	Gay Horton	187	William Reilly
155	David Jacks	188	Josephine Offord
	Elaine Garner		
156	Reginald Waywell		
	Richard Haysom		
157	Alison Jenner		
158	Mary Dixon		

SUDDENLY

Suddenly, without warning,
the texture of my skin seemed coarser,
less sensitive to touch, less supple.
Suddenly the laugh lines
etched deeply on my face
appeared, reflected, more like frowns.
Suddenly, without warning,
my flaxen hair revealed itself more tinged with grey,
less smooth
less tactile.
Suddenly a springtime stroll
became a marathon,
fraught with repercussions,
beset with aches and pains.
Then suddenly, without warning,
you smiled.
My frown lines faded,
and I remembered us.

Leon Rafnson, Dukinfield, Cheshire

Dedicated to Ros who makes me smile and has put up with my ever increasing lines for 38 years.

Leon Rafnson said: "I call myself an Anglo-American, having been born and raised in rural Minnesota, and lived in England since 1971. I am a retired teacher and have been playing with words for as long as I remember. I belong to two writers groups, Writer's Reign and People's Performance, both based in Stalybridge, Cheshire. Both groups have been extremely supportive and helpful, especially when the dreaded "writer's block" sets in. My wife, Ros and I have three daughters and a growing number of grandchildren. We both enjoy reading and the occasional visit to our bungalow in Spain."

TOMORROW IS ANOTHER DAY

The sun can melt the coldest ice
A song can warm the coldest heart
A heart can beat a rhythm
A rhythm can control the pace
The pace of life

The pace of life can be
As cold as ice
As warm as a heartbeat
A rhythm that is slow
A rhythm that is fast
A rhythm ever-changing
Dictating the future
And guarding the past

The past is a part of life
And as we move on
It can be left behind
The future is something
We cannot see
Like an open window
Behind a closed blind

The past can be revisited
The future can be planned
Tomorrow is another day
And time stands still
And life still goes on,
Guided by whose hand?

Diane Stanley, Northwich, Cheshire

HOPE

I hope I can turn out just like my mother
I hope just like her that I'm like no other
I hope for her greatness, her passion, her flair
I hope for her sense to know just what to wear
I hope for her ability to greatly achieve
I hope for her insight to know when to leave
I hope for her huge warm and generous heart
I hope for her confidence to make a new start
I hope for her kindness, her love and her charm
I hope just like her I save people from harm
I hope for the way she sees things to the end
I hope for the ease with which she makes a friend
I hope for her pride in me in all that I do
I hope most of all Mum, I turn out like you

Lynn Alexander, Winwick, Cheshire

MISTER, MY MISTER

Hey Mister, I love you
I thought you should know
My love will stay with you
Wherever you go
You give me strength
In so many ways
You brighten my life
On my darkest of days
You're always there
With sound advice
I guess that is part of
What makes you so nice
I know on you I can depend
You're the love of my life
And my very best friend

Elizabeth Booth, Ellesmere Port, Cheshire

WE ARE ALL JUST PEBBLES ON A BEACH

We are all just pebbles on a beach,
different shapes and sizes
We are not the same, we are unique,
And often full of surprises.

We are all just pebbles on a beach,
none of us are out of reach,
Some lay near rocks and little pools,
just been tossed by the fools.

Pick me up I'm yours to keep,
Or put me down leave me to sleep.
And I'll be cast away once more,
upon that lost and lonely shore.

To be picked up from sands of gold,
yours to have and to hold,
or just put me gently down,
or just leave me here to drown
my sorrows as I gently weep,
I go back to the waters deep.

When the pebbles there washed by the sea,
on the beach there's not only me,
I'm a stranger on the shore,
I'm a stranger not no more.

L J Kirby, Ellesmere Port, Cheshire

BRIGHT ROSE IN MY MIND'S GARDEN

You flower in my mind's garden;
You are the sunshine of my life;
I must ask to beg your pardon,
If I bring to you only strife.

You are my garden's bright, bright rose;
My love's given only to you;
In my heart safe can repose,
As you I love so very true.

Cupid garlands you with flowers
As my mind tells me this is so;
You bring me many happy hours,
In my mind's garden of love, though.

J Millington, Northwich, Cheshire

SEEKING ADA

Think of laughter, think of sincerity.
Remember her telling wise little tales,
Her suddenly serious sympathy;
The sort of assistance that never fails.
Practical home maker, music her dream.
Born into times that were harder than now,
Ada was ready for any good scheme
To help others use gifts God might endow.
Think of home baked buns and strawberry teas,
In the house where friends were happy to meet,
Where chatter was like the buzzing of bees,
For Ada's spirit was round and complete.

Think of music, friendship, gardens and fun.
Your quest for Ada will just have begun

M Munro Gibson, Winsford, Cheshire

SWEETEST

'Cross mountain tops and river flow
Beneath cloud ridden skies
Past meadowlands and valleys low
To a lover he flies

At least a thousand perfumes diffuse
But she is the one he will choose
His heart again he gladly shall lose
Winter sunsets to shades of spring

The torment never dies
Till the moment beats of a wing
Brings him back and she sighs

As the spasms of pleasure begin
His touch like the feathers resting on skin
Probes for the nectar that waits within

The floodgates jar, a final thrust
Pockets all of the prize
Nature thrives, but their world is hushed
When spoken are goodbyes

"I will return," murmurs the honey bee,
To the flower affectionately,
"For you are the sweetest of all to me"

Gary Darbyshire, Warrington, Cheshire

SHARED MOMENTS

Dear friend, today I felt the need
To write a line or two,
To tell you what our friendship means,
And how I treasure you.

You've always been there through the years
To share times, good and bad.
You've laughed with me and cried with me,
Still cheer me when I'm sad.

Do you remember, long ago,
When we were young and free,
What fun we had through schooldays,
And how you shared with me

Those little childhood secrets?
Then later, teenage dreams,
And on to love and motherhood.
How long ago it seems.

Inside my head, I'm still a girl.
Although I'm old and grey,
Remember me, my dear, dear friend.
Yours with affection, Faye.

Eve Armstrong, Warrington, Cheshire

PINK AND BLUE RIBBON

It was always springtime in Annie's room
With a vase of fresh flowers ever in bloom
An oriental carpet on the plain wooden floor
Polished with beeswax the furniture and door

A bundle of letters in the chest of drawers
Each season she placed a sprig of lavender
Lovingly tied with a pink and blue ribbon
Marking his memory in her heart's calendar

Reading his letters that came from France
He wrote with fondness of their last tea dance
And hoped to be home with joy and no tears
The picture on the shelf never aged with the years

Leonard Pettifer, Wilmslow, Cheshire

CALL FOR ME

Call for me
And take me to your dreams
That is where I belong
Shush, you say
Please don't make a noise

Then we hold each other's hand
And float off into the sky

How breathtaking it was
To be with you throughout the night
Soaring like two birds
I, very truly under your wing
Safe I am when I am with you
Oh if only I could not wake up

Eileen Baxter-Percival, Warrington, Cheshire

YASMIN

God looked down upon us
And from heaven above
He sent us an angel
For us all to love

Ten tiny fingers
Ten tiny toes
Big brown eyes
And a button nose

Brown curly hair
And olive skin
Two little dimples
And a cheeky grin

Mummy and daddy made
A special little girl
With a big bright smile
And little curls

God looked down
From heaven above
And sent us an angel
For us all to love

Dot Reese, Northwich, Cheshire

ONE DAY

One day I fell in your ocean
gripped by the whirlpool I made
when the world is torn and flowing
I gasp the dampest serenade
reduced with each look and thought
Angel, will your sweetness fade?

One day I gazed at the twilight,
the last light played on your face,
I held your warm and absent hand
but sat alone in the darkest place,
where flowers bloom around me
but cut me so far from your grace.

Richard Trotter, Chester, Cheshire

MOON FROST

Moonfrost illuminating the air,
With coldings of ice.
Moonfrost I wish for nothing finer
Than for you to be, tonight.
Moonfrost I wish I were a miner
Digging for your silver
Amidst clouded caves, in the sky.

Moonfrost freezing all you touch
With incandescent lunar ecstasy.
Moonfrost or cold, shimmering witch
You are as beautiful as death.
Moonfrost queen so regally reserved,
In ermines of lunar white,
You're so unlike the vulgar *demos* of summer.

Martin Jenkins, Ellesmere Port, Cheshire

MY FOUR LEGGED FRIEND

As I look in your eyes
I see how you care
When I stretch out my hand
You're always there

Without question you listen
When I'm feeling low
And the secrets I tell you
No other will know

With love and attention
Food and a walk
Your tail wags when happy
There's no need for talk

I'll be there to protect you
Right to the end
As you're there for me
My four-legged friend

Dawn Hough, Northwich, Cheshire

*Dedicated to my husband Steve whose bond with our
Alsation, Scorch, inspired me to write my four legged friend.*

I DON'T WANT TO BE FAMOUS

I don't want to be famous,
I just want to be loved,
I don't want to be beautiful,
I just want to be hugged,
I don't want cold cleverness,
Or mocking, biting wit,
If knocking down is how you build,
I want no part of it,
I just want to cuddle,
When it's raining, and it's cold,
And maybe share a dream or two,
With someone I can hold.

Matthew Entwistle, Warrington, Cheshire

THE GREATEST GIFT

This letter is so difficult to write, from your grief has come
our joy,
Through the loss of your child, you gave us back our boy,
As I cradle my child, warm with life we thought would soon
be gone,
We'll be forever in your debt, for what you have both done.
In your grief you made the hardest decision any parents
could make,
Allowing your child's heart to be used, for another's sake,
His tiny heart, beats in our son's body each day,
The life force which enables our son to play,
You both gave and took, without any self-gain,
In giving our child life, you took away our pain,
We ask ourselves would we have done the same?
Would we have cared for a stranger without a name?
Each day of our son's life, I will give thanks and pause,
And reflect on your kindness, affectionately yours.

Denise Baines, Hyde, Cheshire

WHEN I LOOK AT YOU

When I look at you
I see a man with love lit eyes
Looking back at me
A smile mischievously playing
On your lips
Lips to kiss again and again
Deliciously searching, imploring lips
Which fit mine perfectly,

When I look at you
A look is never enough
Touching your face
Arms around you
Fingers exploring your skin
Delving deep beneath your layers
Our fingers interlock
Like our eyes exchanging precious moments
Arms and legs entwined
Bodies twisted, squashing the existing air away
Deeply penetrating personal space to find
A place of comfort together, becoming the other, existing as
one.

Stephanie Dickinson, Northwich, Cheshire

YOUNG LOVE

A young man's fancy so they say
Turns to romance in the spring
Young girls all aglow look out for a beau
And long for a show of affection
As nature blossoms and springs to life
Young lovers to a wedding are going
Full of delight, what a wonderful sight to behold
Be their chief guest, Lord
Lord of all loving, Lord of all living
This wedding day
Bind them together in your sure keeping
Husband and wife on this special spring day

Gladys Rhodes, Dukinfield, Cheshire

SIGNAL PROBLEMS (AFTER A VISIT TO MY AUNT)

Sitting in the this train, waiting, waiting,
"We apologise for the delay,
Free tea and coffee is available from"
I get up,
Until,
"Come on train, come on"

On a high bank I see,
(Or think I see), old men's beards,
And knobbly trees with camels' tails
Lifting upwards to the sky.
Very weird indeed.

And I think of you,
Now a long way away,
Knowing how the knot of time is passing
Like daisies in the distant fields.

Maureen Weldon, Chester, Cheshire

24

THE HANDIWORK OF GOD

Some people sing of romance, wax lyrical for hours,
But I prefer to write about a garden full of flowers.
For romance may be fleeting
And a heart may thus be broken,
Cupid's arrow missed its mark,
Though words of love were spoken.

Romantic love is fickle, here today and gone tomorrow,
Unrequited passion leads to loneliness and sorrow.
But a garden brings fulfilment, never ceases to astound,
As never-ending miracles come sprouting from the ground.

Wordsworth wrote of daffodils dancing in the breeze,
Keats and many others told of pleasures such as these.
The presence of a greater force is there for all to see,
In the petals of a daisy or a tall majestic tree.

Though many sing of romance, as previously stated,
I think it's past its sell-by-date, and greatly overrated.
How reciprocal a pleasure as I tend my garden plot,
With loving care it blossoms forth and disappoints me not.

Diana Burrows, Weaverham, Cheshire

THE BRACELET

The gift from a soldier
A gold bracelet lay on the stall
of the local charity sale
A gift of love to his loved one
many years ago
Days past by! years passed by.
I fear he has not returned.
The bond of the bracelet
for happy years to come
Tears of joy have turned to
sorrow the button from his
tunic is all that is left to mourn

Edna Fallowfield, Chester, Cheshire

BURIED ALIVE

Death in the restaurant, the dining dead,
Opposite one another we sit, head to head,
Looking everywhere but there.
Engrossed, deeply engrossed in the à la carte,
Fascinated by the words swimming on the page,
Weighing up the merits of prawn cocktail and melon balls.
It bores the soul to sit, surrounded by strangers.
Strange why we even bother to perform cupid's ritual.
Yet here we are again. More wine? More bread?
Forget forced politeness, we're already dead.
Searching for something not on the menu,
Conversation revolves.
We rise to leave and he helps me on with my coat,
Kisses my cheek,
Public affection number one.
Death in the doorway, the only way out.
I rise.

Laura Anne Douglas, Warrington, Cheshire

SNAPSHOTS IN TIME

There are no exams in preparation
And even when you think you've swotted up
There is no formal inauguration
And yet sweet is the celebration cup
Raised in that ecstactic moment in time
When you first touch your babe, joy is sublime

On sun soaked beaches are people who laugh and call
Unsuspecting as earth cracks, slides 'neath ocean's floor
Arms flay wildly, vanish, as water smothers all
And tears falling like rain, mourn those who are no more

As summer sun sinks slowly in the West
And sun meets ocean, reflections fireball
Puts every other beauteous thing to test
As explosive colour infuses all

Events nine eleven and tsunami
Have shown that the play is on chequered boards
Still, though crystal clear you will never be
Dear life, I remain affectionately yours

Liz Standish, Warrington, Cheshire

IT'S ME

It's me!
Here I am
Brand spanking new.
I tell you it's true.
I've re-programmed my reticular system,
Re-jigged my body and brain.
I'm re-designed, re-organised and re-calibrated:
Riddled myself of all things outdated.
I have new understandings, feelings, thoughts and ideas.
Old beliefs have gone and I have no fears.
I know who I am
And the reason I'm here.

Rosemary Graham, Nantwich, Cheshire

MEG

Happiness is hearing you rush to the door,
Our ritual dance makes me smile.
Leaping, bouncing, soggy greetings never fail.
Never angry, always forgiving for time spent away,
You follow me around as though I'm Little Bo-Peep,
Your eyes bright and dewy, waiting for the signal,
That food is on the way.

Happiness is seeing your coat shine, fox red in the
sunshine.
Listening to your animated dreams. Feet twitching,
Jowls rumbling as excited growls indicate
Rabbits being chased across spring green fields.
Your dreams only interrupted by the sound of a misplaced
Squeaky toy, being trodden on. You snap awake, leaping
onto, the chewed plastic ball, ready to play.

Annie Morrisey, Betley, Cheshire

LONELY RIVERS

Lonely rivers and clear blue skies,
I can see the world through your eyes.

Our last meeting holds fast inside my mind,
Recalling feelings I did not mean to find,
Walking through valleys of deep emerald green,
I witnessed sights no one else has seen.
You let go of the horse's tether,
And whispered the words that will last forever.

My eyes flew open in the middle of this dream,
As I realised there were no valleys of emerald green,
Only one dusty street to tell the tale,
Of that winter evening our love set sail.
Out of the darkness I saw your pale lips smile,
You once told me that it wasn't your style.

No amount of valleys and wild horses will make me stay,
Only being the man that you are today.
Lonely rivers and clear blue skies,
I can see the world through your eyes.

Gemma Connell, Wilmslow, Cheshire

THINK HAPPY TIMES

When dearest friends have gone away
You have to try to fill each day
The grief you have so deep inside
Sometimes you feel you want to hide
But just remember happier times
Before the tears of all the smiles
The jokes we had, the pranks we played
Sharing of thoughts our crazy ideas
A long true friendship of many years
At times I feel you are so near
I can't believe you are not here

Celia Cholmondeley, Warrington, Cheshire

FOREVER

They have tried to crush my spirit,
But I'll still come to you,
For you are my light, my hopes and dreams,
And at night, when all is quiet,
I am in that land of sunshine and laughter
Where you are?

Their attitude torments me,
They say I'm wrong and stupid, not good enough,
I am filled with love, and they are full of hate,
What gives them the right to take away my dreams?
Don't tell me they are happy,
Because I don't believe it.

And so my love, against all odds,
I will bathe in the sunlight of your love.
I am with you, our souls entwined
And spirits go on forever.

Christine Rowley, Winterley, Cheshire

ODE TO GENTLEMAN TED

At three months old I bought you
You stole my heart and drove me mad
With endless tricks and games of chase
Your elegance and sleek blue coat
With long whiptail and bright green eyes
Attracted smiles from all you met

Then came a shock at your first show
With "Best in Show" you staggered me
A kitten still at five months plus
You're full of charm and wickedness
From strength to strength at every show
Till premiership at birthday one

The judges love you so do I
I'm hoping for "Grand Premier" soon
Then no more shows to travel to
I sometimes feel you're wrongly named
And could more aptly be called
My very own blue Teddy Boy

Doreen Nall, Chester, Cheshire

JEAN

Friendship is forever, not to flit away,
It's being there for someone each and every day.
A gesture made between us, a nod, a wink, a grin,
Can only be read by those who we let in.
To care about another, just knowing they are fine,
An arm around a shoulder and the odd glass of wine.
Genuine excitement when things are going right,
Make a good friendship, even the odd fight.
I guess I want to say to you, I love you Jean my friend,
A strong-willed fiery person, a true friend till the end.

Susan Griffiths, Crewe, Cheshire

SELF

A head burned cold outside the door,
The chill casts its own spell.
Its eggshell casing cracked on the floor,
The mind blisters where it fell.

This linen made it feel worse,
Like a quadraplegic in hell,
But from this violent ripping birth
I can wrestle with myself.

Why? This person has no role.
I hope to God that they cannot tell.
Each new day lays siege to this hole,
Have I ever felt so well?

I'm seeing more than I want to be shown
Yet if I dull it I cannot tell.
So I'm stupefied on the side of the road,
I just want to crawl back into myself.

Damian Mitchell, Crewe, Cheshire

LOVE AND LOST

We wed just thirty years ago when life and love were new,
Travelling along life's highway, the skies were always blue.
Together we laughed, together we cried,
Never apart, side by side.
After three years wed to my pride and joy,
I gave birth to a baby boy.
Congratulations came from here and there,
Never was there such a happy pair.
As time marched on, in my heart, no song,
I suddenly felt something was wrong.
What can it be? What is amiss?
Tenderness gone from his goodnight kiss.
Heartbroken, I guess our marriage was dead,
He confessed he'd found someone else to wed.
He sent me a card from distant shores,
No love, of course, just "Affectionately yours",
What went wrong? I'm filled with despair,
Oh how I loved him, it just isn't fair.
Single once more, my world's full of rain,
God willing I'll learn to love again.

Lesbia Mary Shone, Little Neston, Cheshire

CHATTERBOX

Why did I ever teach you to speak?
The effort I made week after week
The praises we gave when you coped with a verb
Someone had gone, not "gonned" we heard

My mother did warn me you'd never shut up
Then it was "Daddy gone", "Where teddy?", "Where cup?"
As soon as I mastered your "telegraph speech"
It was on to the next stage I had to teach

You talked and you talked then you went to school
And still you kept talking, free rein was the rule
You talked about books, music and toys
Then suddenly one day, you talked about boys

The place was so quiet once you had gone
Now you are married with your own little son
Thank goodness I think as I teach him to talk
Shout and demand for his spoon or his fork

Dorothy Webster, Chester, Cheshire

TOGETHER AGAIN

Apart so long,
I know not how I lasted.
Such a distance,
This old heart is passed it.
But now you're next to me
The purpose I can see,
For such a separation
Oh joy, what reparations,
What payment for my pain
Now you are back again.

Dawn Adams, Warrington, Cheshire

FORTY YEARS

You're my waking, my sleeping,
Each breath that I take,
You're my reason for living,
You're my reason to wake,
You're the sun in my day,
You're the stars in my night,
You make my life whole,
You make everything right,
There isn't a second of a single day,
You don't bring me joy,
In every way.
You hold my soul within your hand
To cherish, to love until the end,
I shall love you always,
As I do today.
My love for you won't go away.
It's been too long,
It's been too deep,
And so my love,
It's yours to keep.

Elizabeth Livesey, Golborne, Cheshire

HAIKU: END OF AN ERA

A little light breeze,
Flying ashes sting the eye
Memories of mum.

Diane Davy, Nantwich, Cheshire

THE WAY LOVE OUGHT TO BE

When I hold you close to me,
So near, I feel so warm,
You seem to feel the same way,
Love like a summer storm.

When I whisper that I love you,
You answer me, the same,
You mean to me, so much I feel
A passion deep inflamed.

True, love comes to everyone
At some time in their lives
Find the feelings deep enough
For no secrets to hide.

I've never really felt true love,
Never fulfilled my fantasy,
To feel a love so strong and just
The way love ought to be.

Stephen Flinn, Crewe, Cheshire

TOGETHERNESS

Our strength is our togetherness and together,
We are strong, we smile at scented potpourri,
See plastic bottle shaped like swans.

Our love is our togetherness and together in love,
We're strong, our togetherness years have
Shown us both, we know where we belong.

Our life is our togetherness and our togetherness
Is our bond, our affection shines a symphony,
As we sail on golden ponds. And sailing in our

Rowing boat, one day we'll see our eternal dawn,
Where togetherness shall remain our strength
And where together we'll be reborn.

And where forever we'll smile at potpourri and
See plastic bottles shaped like swans, gliding
Beside our rowing boat, as we sail on chosen ponds.

Kevin O'Brien, Warrington, Cheshire

Dedicated to my Ruth - love always.

MY BEST FRIEND

I look into your grape green eyes
And I see the most prestigious prize
As my very being wells with emotion,
I see a lifetime of love and devotion.

As you place your weary head in my lap
The time spent together I can now recap.
Everyone learnt about your wonderful story
I am sorry for the fame and the glory.

I know you only wanted to be by my side
I watch you breathe and smile with pride.
You are my sunshine after the rain,
You make me smile, you ease my pain.

And, yes, sadly, you will leave me one day
Inevitably, there is one thing I must say,
Tabby Tiger, from the bottom of my heart, Thank you.
Oh, best friend puss, was that a mew? I love you too.

Theresa M Carrier, Davenham, Cheshire

TALK TO ME

Come down to the waterside
In timeless ebb and flow
Bathe your feelings wonderings
And let your beauty grow.

Shoulder for your weeping whim
A cradle unrestrained
A kindred mind, an open ear
In confidence sustained.

For you may never know at all
Unless words intertwine
That silent care, sincere unbound
Poor open heart of mine.

And who's to call you right or wrong
Expose you or deny
I offer you a love that's free
If only you would try.

Philip John Savage, Macclesfield, Cheshire

DARKNESS

Darkness falls around me and yet I lie awake
The third time this week, it's just too much to take
The worries of the world inside my head
Cannot be faced by me in bed.

Somehow I feel responsible, why should I
Take the blame for all those who choose to cry?
Why must the world be screwed up like this?
Accepting fear and godlessness.

It's not my fault but still I know
The pain afflicting this world so
The words of hate but reasons lost
The greed of many to what cost.

And so I lie forlorn and mad
At how the world could be so bad
If only they sorted out worldly things
I'd get the sleep the darkness brings

Christopher Johnson, Anderton, Cheshire

THERE IS HOPE

Don't be worried by negative circumstances
Your money or rather your extravagances
Your prominent position in this world today
Or if people persecute you along life's way

Bureaucrats who make life difficult for you
Intimidation and cynicism flourish anew
The Lord can alter and make a transformation
Optimism will emerge, you will come out of depression

Be convinced of the existence of his power
He can be with you night and day, hour by hour
It is not easy, you need exceeding self-control
You will incur spiritual opposition, that's the devil's role

The power of the Lord can certainly overcome
God gave a lot of his power to his only son
Jesus loves you no matter what you have done
He will hold out his hands and say, "Come child come"

Sylvia M Harbert, Warrington, Cheshire

BONFIRES

Soft wind traipses through,
Trembles through spring-budded branches
Reaches out to puff red
The embers
To sweep fragrant smoke
In delicate curls.

Leaves that surrendered
That fell crisp-brown to autumn's kiss
Shudder to weightless cinders.
Their veins
Like the crocheted thread of dreams
Splintered to dust.

Tight-bellied buds peer down
Clustered close, warmed by sun,
Feeling for life's first rewards
Balefully, staring out the
Blackened earth
Without knowing.

Rob Farley, Knutsford, Cheshire

TRULY BLESSED

When I was young
and love was new
our hearts beat together
my hand in yours
our love was strong
and each day we treasured

The seasons came the seasons went
and wed we did become
to share our love
throughout the years
united we are one

The little church upon the hill
has stood there year by year
today today we celebrate
thirty years out measured

The vicar with his flowing gown
is here today to bless us
the congregation clapped and cheered
as we announced
our love together

Margery Rayson, Ulverston, Cumbria

THEY LIVE

As long as I'm alive
They live in me,
The people I have known.
I think of them,
Remembering,
And find I'm not alone.

Julia Dent, Kirkby Stephen, Cumbria

WORDS OF LOVE

The days are long and dark when you're not there
To care,
I long to hold you close, to have you near,
To hear
Your words of love so sweet, I need your kiss,
Such bliss,
Please let me feel once more your tenderness,
Caress
Me with your hands so gentle, hold me tight,
The night
Is lonely without you, I need your touch
So much,
I think of you each moment you're away,
Each day,
So just remember what I said, I do
Love you.

Pat Porter, Carlisle, Cumbria

THE LOVE OF MY LIFE

Since I met you, my whole life's changed,
You've made it worth my while.
'Cause every time I look at you,
I see that special smile.

You're there for me through thick and thin,
And always say you care.
I never thought I'd find someone,
With my life I'd want to share.

I never dreamed that I could be,
As happy as I am.
Or feel the love I feel inside,
But now I know I can.

So just remember all my love,
I give to you with pleasure.
And everything that we go through,
My heart will always treasure.

Lorena Sandwith, Maryport, Cumbria

Dedicated to Stuart Hutchinson, the love of my life.

THANKS FOR BEING THERE

I write these words to you, in my own special way
Thanking you for your help, over many years
Comforting words, standing alongside, every day
Helping me smile, forbidding the cascading of tears

Your attractive smile, those engaging eyes
You were attentive, when I needed, to bare my soul
Though I no longer, have to unburden my cries
Inside of me, remains a tremendous hole.

With tormented mind, you stood by my side
My demons, you wished to ensnare
Encouragement given, you would never deride
My guardian angel, always there, with such care.

Your resoluteness, always shone through
Like a diamond, at night, shining in the sky
A loyal and trusted friend, you have always been true
When I think of you, my eyes are never dry.

We've both moved on, though we often speak
It always hurts, when we both say, goodbye
Your strength stimulated me, when I was weak
It's only you, to whom this dedication, does apply.

Brian Brailey, Whitehaven, Cumbria

AN ANNIVERSARY GIFT

It was our first wedding anniversary
At four thirty, very early in the morn
That a beautiful six pound, half ounce baby
Girl first saw the light of dawn.

She was the most precious gift in every way;
Like all babies, well worth the long wait.
Fate must have decreed she was born that day
As she was actually four and a half hours late.

She's a dear daughter, mother, nanna and wife;
Her concern for others ever in mind,
And that's how it's been throughout her life.
She is caring, loving and kind.

She is not by any means an only child;
Her two brothers, one sadly gone to his rest,
Were and are just as caring, loving and kind.
In our children we've been truly most blest.

Marlene Allen, Penrith, Cumbria

MY FRIEND, THE BLADE

You were my best friend,
Once upon a time
Thankfully I've outgrown you
But I still remember
Because my body bears the marks
The scars left by your caress
I loved you and needed it
My only escape was your sting
However, I've moved on
I see you for the friend you were
Just a blight upon my skin

Lee Rose, Carlisle, Cumbria

OUR STAR

Our daughter died age twenty three
We don't know why this had to be
Each day I kiss her photograph and stroke her tiny cheek
I tell her that I love her and someday we all will meet
She was a very happy girl, so kind and full of life
Her friends gave her a star one night
To shine down from above
It is the brightest one you see, it's sending us her love
I know it is our daughter's star, it sparkles oh so bright
She sparkled when she lived on earth
And now she sparkles every night
Oh how I love this precious sight
No greater gift have we received
No one can ever take away
This precious star is here to stay
Affectionately ours forever mam and dad

Brenda Wood, Cockermouth, Cumbria

LEARNING

No-one in our family was considered very bright.
We paid our way and did a job and tried to do it right.
Yet here you are at college taking a degree
With all those other boys and girls far cleverer than me
It makes me proud to think that you are putting up a fight

When I was young and bosses said "your wages will be cut"
We went on strike, we always lost. the factory was shut.
But you can find another post because you can adapt
To other types of work out there where futures can be
tapped.
My generation lost because we stayed deep in a rut.

All this learning baffles me, I can't tell what you say
Yet someone does, for five years on, we've reached a final
day
When in a gown and funny hat, certificate in hand,
You smile at the photographer exactly as you planned,
While I beam at my grandson, B Sc (Hons), M B A.

Richard Clark, Penrith, Cumbria

ON THE BUS

I saw you on the bus today:
I wish I knew your name.
You never even looked my way;
I love you just the same.

You sit alone with no-one near:
I yearn to be your friend.
Your lips, your cheeks, your hair, your ear,
I love the thoughts they send.

I'd like to save you from a bear,
Slay dragons just for you,
Climb mountains, swim to Finisterre,
And pilot Concorde too.

But then, I'm twelve, you're seventeen:
I'm reaching for the moon.
My love will still stay evergreen
Till Monday: See you soon.

Anthony Payne, St Bees, Cumbria

HOME TOWN

My belonging uplifts me, my spirit nourishes me
I cling like a child to its mother
Sad to leave, glad to return
Melancholy for those who could not stay
Once there stood a college
Grand mansion only Victorian gates remain rusting
Miners hewed coal for industry
Still standing the red sandstone home of my childhood
But gone the feather bed with soft white pillows
In the attic room smelling of dried lavender
Where sunlight streamed through the skylight
Making a spotlight full of sparkle

Ann Douglas-Kedwell, Aspatria, Cumbria

A SONG ON THE BREEZE

A song on the breeze,
My heart is uplifted -
A cloud in the sky:
A lyrical melody drifting, singing
Oh, lingering dream,
Your spirit of beauty
A voice of the night
Echoing silence ... whispering
The music of dreams,
A child who is smiling,
The mystery of moonlight,
Souls awak'ning -
Angels of harmony
Ah ...
A fount of peace,
Love and joy to the world!

Carol Smith, Keswick, Cumbria

THE NEW ARRIVAL

He came to us.
A seedling blown on the wind.
"Just a couple of days," they said.
"I love you," he said.
"You can't," I said.
But he did.

The seed was sown.
Roots burrowed into our minds and hearts.
The tendrils grew, encircled our lives.
"I love you," he said.
But he did.

Weeks flourished on, into months.
He stayed and grew strong.
Trust and respect flowered profusely.
"Do you love me?", he said.
"Yes we do!", we said.
And we did!

Jillian Minion, Millom, Cumbria

THANK YOU

Thank you for every seed you sow
Thank you for everyone I know
You made my eyes, ears and nose
You tied my hair with pretty bows
Upon your land I was placed
Upon your being I was based
From you I've learnt so many things
From you I've grown great golden wings
A root of length
A root of strength
The power of strife
The power of life
Thank you for every seed you sow
Thank you for everyone I know

Lynn Hamel, Kendal, Cumbria

LITTLE SISTER'S BIRTHDAY

Greetings on your birthday to you sister dear,
The day that once did change the seasons of the year,
Birds sang sweet songs, skies were bright upon that happy morn,
For spring came in December the day that you were born.

Though far away from home I've strayed, I find the darkest days
Are bright, when I remember your smile and sunny ways,
Though the years pass by, and even time grows old
Birds will sing for you, the sun shine his brightest gold.
Your heart will hold but happiness and youth, all this I know,
Because, like all who know you, sweet girl, I love you so.

Barbara Newton, Grange-over-Sands, Cumbria

SOMEONE LIKE YOU

Searching,
For peace
Contentment and trust,
Needing,
Mans love
Optimism and security.
Yearning,
For justice
Truth over lies.
Hoping,
For friendship
Lasting and true.
Praying,
For love
Someone like you.
Saved,
Forever,
I thank you

Jeanette Cort, Glenridding, Cumbria

ALWAYS

When I needed you to be with me, stay with me, support me,
Were you there?
When friends rebuked me, hurt me, misunderstood me,
Did you care?
When we disagreed, argued, conflicted, exchanged views,
Were you fair?
When life was good to us, lucky for us, joyful for us, kind to us,
Did you share?
In happy times, sad times, good times and bad times,
Were you there?
Always!
Always my constant companion,
Always my loving champion.
Always with me even when apart,
Always and ever in my soul and in my heart.

Carole Somerville, Penton, Cumbria

MUM

We hope you like it as it comes
To us, we call it love
You are our mum to whom we give
It all from up above

We think just of you daily
And from all around
You are always in our heart
And in flowers on the ground

But because you are so special
You're always in our heart
We never want to be away from you mum
We'll never be apart

Julia Lawrence, Barrow-in-Furness, Cumbria

WILL I EVER SMILE?

Will I ever feel the sun on my face?
Will I ever look up and smile?
I cannot see beyond my tears,
Since the day you died,
They tell me you are all around,
In the wind that blows,
Or a bird that flies so high,
But I cannot see beyond my tears,
For now I am truly blind,
When my tears have washed all pain away,
I may,
Look up and smile.

Elizabeth Latter, Barrow-in-Furness, Cumbria

Dedicated to my husband Ron Latter who died 3rd June 2004. My one true love.

JENNIFER

We do not always see eye to eye
I know I interfere
What mother wouldn't?
I try to save you pain,
The heart break, which makes you cry

I have been there, before you
Wearing your shoes
Maybe different circumstances
The outcome the same
Which left me feeling blue

In my mind I worry about you more
Any mother would
No matter your age
A mother is for life
My daughter I am affectionately yours

Sheila Drewery, Barrow-in-Furness, Cumbria

FIFTY YEARS TOGETHER

I don't think I was the perfect wife
To you, in all our years.
I may have strayed occasionally or given into fears.
But you were always there for me
You loved our family dear.
Steadfast, so reliable
Your faith was strong and clear.
You became so ill, in later years.
And needed me to care
You brought out all my love for you
And I was always there.
But now you've gone. I'm on my own
Still faithful to our memories,
Oh, How the years have flown.

Rita Lancaster, Barrow-in-Furness, Cumbria

SMILE

Oh day. Don't pass away until I find a kindly smile.
Don't ever come and leave my face in pain
Don't ever come and let me have a thought defiled
Never will you fade, where a saddened eye leave a stain.

What be a day if happiness passes not, on it's way.
Where a smile has been lost, and face it, has not crossed.
It comes never stays. sure of not another day.
T'is a gift to life, has no price or cost.

Is that not a sight, does the sun not smile so bright;
Lift the day for you to smile, in a contagious way?
For as the sun melts its light, to late, it's night,
Oh. Never let a day, without a smile, go away.

Alan Green, Castleton, Greater Manchester

SEALED WITH A LOVING KISS

No words,
No thoughts,
No wildest dreams:
Only her.

Simon Bostock, Stockport, Greater Manchester

THE WILD SIDE OF THE WIFE

Don't rock the boat if sailing smooth,
I've often heard it said,
But I am in the dog house,
And the wife is seeing red.
I came in late one evening
Far the worst for drink,
She said your supper's in the kitchen,
In the waste bin near the sink.
So up to bed I wobbled,
And no words did come my way,
But boy how did I suffer
When I woke up next day.
Breakfast was took in silence,
And dinner was the same,
She made it clear throughout the day,
That I was to blame.
She never spoke a single word,
And that cut me like a knife,
Thank God it's not often, that I see,
The wild side of the wife.

Ian David Hogg, Heywood, Greater Manchester

HE WHO DARES WINS?

The gathering of men, a meeting of minds,
As we initiate our next attack,
On a crusade for our country, a frenzy of fighting patriots,
Any thought of defeat or death we appear to lack.

We advance forward engaged in banter and bravado,
Two by two, we keep apace.
Although, some seem unsettled in the knowledge
That the same footsteps they will never retrace.

As we draw closer to the symphony of shells
And bullets that tear through the air.
The corporals countdown reaches its climax. and
We take cover without a moment to spare.

However, some friends fumble to the ground but not of
their own accord,
As we wonder whether, "he who dares, wins?"
Whilst bombardments beckon and bulldoze the last stand
of soldiers
Like a bowling ball pulverising its pins.

But suddenly all is silent, no last draw of breath can be
heard,
No faint shudder or move is made.
And I too lay lifeless in the hope of suffering a similar fate,
Wanting to be dead rather than the only one saved.

Danny Noctor-Patton, Rochdale, Greater Manchester

MY SPECIAL FRIEND

Brian is my special friend
I chat to him online
He always brightens up my day
He is thoughtful, nice and kind
He is always there when I need him for advice, a laugh, a
hug
It is great when I can meet him
In fact it is very good
We are hoping it gets better
Sharing lots of things
But we will have to wait and see, what tomorrow brings.

Gloria Hamlett, Swinton, Greater Manchester

Dedicated to Brian, my special friend, thanks mate.

VALENTINE GREETING

Would you be my valentine
My partner throughout life?
Would you be my valentine
And one day be my wife?

I will go down on bended knee
To pledge my love for you
And treat you with great respect
To prove my love for you

I cannot say enough my dear
You break my heart in two
My thoughts are all about you
In everything I do

Ann Noble, Stockport, Greater Manchester

GEORGE

I pen this poem to you,
I remember it was Summer time,
And I had just picked some sage and thyme,

A cottage garden to behold,
With lots of stories to be told,
Colours of red, blue and green, were forever to be seen,

The cottage with thatched roof was old,
But many stories it did hold,
Pale white walls and deep blue door,
Opened to a welcome, overlooking the shore,

Stepping down from gate to sea,
That is when I first saw thee,
Strong and handsome, you were my beau,
Oh, dear George, why did you go.

Now I'm aged but I know,
My best friend loved me so,
Four great paws and sorrowful eyes,
But you were so wise,
Affectionately yours, I will be,
At the thatched cottage, by the sea.

Denise Sonia Ogden, Bolton, Greater Manchester

IN YOUR ARMS

With warmth and security
Love and trust
My life is in your hands
And this is a must

I don't really know why
I think like I do
But to be in your arms
Is a dream come true

With kisses and cuddles
And your gentle voice
My head on your shoulder
Makes my heart rejoice

I dribble and giggle
(a gurgling sound)
You hug and caress me
(I like what I've found)

You kiss me and stroke me
There's no harm in that
For I am in bliss
I'm only your cat.

Sandra Hawarden-Lord, Rochdale, Greater Manchester

GARDEN OF PRAYER

I often visit
The garden of prayer,
Physically,
Or imagine I'm there.

Breathing in peace,
And calm of the air,
A secret blessing,
Awaits for me there.

Pauline Y Whitworth, Wigan, Greater Manchester

THREE PART HARMONY

A glance; a touch; so sweet a kiss.
Was ever love as pure as this?

Five dates; soul mates; true romance.
No others I had dated really stood a chance.
Hearts bound; bliss found; search complete.
This unfamiliar feeling swept me off my feet.

A sigh; a tear; a parting hiss.
Was ever pain as raw as this?

No dates; no mates; life on hold.
Submerged in sad reflection of a love gone cold.
Teeth ground; eyes drowned; incomplete.
Night battles with the pillow ending in defeat.

A smile; a sigh; "I really miss."
United in a life of bliss.

Marylyn Blackshaw, Rochdale, Greater Manchester

WITH A GAZE

Communication from the eyes
As with a gaze we hold
Silence in transmission
But feelings clearly hold

A thousand words enfolding
Reflection of your thoughts
Unspoken but yet given
Precious gems not sought

The message is affection
For one that we hold dear
To say I'm yours forever
And it's good to have you near

For many years we've waited
This moment to enjoy
The prodigal returning
As an adult not a boy

The bond of love not broken
But given time and space
Revealing now a vein of gold
The love upon your face

Margaret Rose, Wigan, Greater Manchester

HELP FROM THE WEATHER

I feel your pain across the wind,
The birds they sing your sorrow,
The leaves they flutter and dance around,
Spelling your name with a stutter.
The lightening strikes, the thunder roars,
The beating rain explains.
You feel I've strayed and let you down,
Yet I love no other.
Be still my beating heart I say,
Be true and tell the sun,
To carry my love on rays of light,
And bring us back as one.

Carol Edith Hopgood, Bolton, Greater Manchester

LOSS

Here and there I look for you
Round every tree I peep for you
Along each road I walk with you
Each path I tread I follow you
Each hour of the day I think of you
Each thought I have is just for you
Each road I drive searches for you
Everywhere I go my reason is you

How does it feel to hold such power?
To know I think of you every hour
Do you ever think of me this way
And do you look for me and say
What of my life now you're not there
Along life's lonely road?
Where will I be when this road ends
Without you my life to share?

Val J Chapman, Rochdale, Greater Manchester

MY FRIEND JOYCE

A friend's love is always there for you
Whatever the demands great or few
Through all life's many ups and downs
Her care and support would be found

A shoulder to cry on, a hug we would share
You've listened and helped and always been there
Nothing too much trouble for you
Friends like you are special and few

So here we are good friends together
Nothing will part us we're here forever
As time goes by we might not admit
To the grey, the glasses and clothes that won't fit

You're part of my life and friends we'll stay
We've shared and cared and that's our way
As the years go by and whatever life sends
I'm glad that we are such special friends

So may God guide you on your way
And watch over you every night and day
All this and more I ask for you
Blessings to last your whole life through

Sandra Mooney, Stockport, Greater Manchester

A LETTER TO MY DAD

Dad, you had slipped away when I wrote this,
I held your hand, but it's your cuddle I miss.
We really do need you right here,
To join in the fun, the mirth and the cheer.

It was mid-September when your bright light faded,
Nothings stayed in my mind like that day did.
I've never stopped missing you, not even today.
I miss your laughter and funny things you'd say.

My daddy has died and left me alone,
You'll never see how my children have grown.
We'll never go walking again on the moors,
But I'll always remain affectionately yours.

Rebecca Davis, Bury, Greater Manchester

WORDS

The words were hidden inside her head
A poem which started with an idea
The thoughts and words did spread
And how they needed to be said

Should she speak them aloud?
And let them disappear forever
Wrapped in a passing cloud
Taken and jumbled together

Or
Should she write them down?
Their shape and form to be
A poem to be read
And saved for all posterity

Sheila Ellis, Prestwich, Greater Manchester

WHAT IS A BULLY?

Someone who waits
Until he sees weakness.
Then by instinct
Races in, making his killing.

Knowing the other doesn't know
What he is doing.
The other simply wallows
In turmoil and confusion.

The other finds isolation
Blames himself most.
For the doer is his "friend"
He couldn't hurt him.

One day he'll know
The poison of his "friend."
But that poisons gone too deep
Better leave him.

The bully is someone
Who struggles with himself.
Bullying he thinks a brave thing
And all else is worthless.

Prakash Solanki, Ashton-under-Lyne, Greater Manchester

TIME IS RUNNING OUT

Can you love me as I am?
Can you accept me now, the way I am?
Or, have we lost the bond we had?
Or is it that we're both still scared and sad?

Is it time to let go and settle for just being friends?
Or do we keep fighting to hold on to the very end?
Why does the decision have to be left with me?
My promise stayed true, I'll always love you endlessly.

But I can't be with you, if emotions are not returned the same,
Leaving myself open, to be hurt over and over again.
Time is running out.

Jo Rainford, Leigh, Greater Manchester

DEAR BOBBY

I left you at the airport,
With no time to say, "Goodbye."
You said you'd send a postcard,
Phone every other day.

Without you, the sun withdrew
To louring clouds of grey,
You did not send a message
And the sad hours ticked away.

But now my heart is lighter,
You phoned me yesterday.
You miss your home, your mother,
Will come back on Saturday.

Hazel Wellings, Leigh, Greater Manchester

YOU ARE

You are my polaroid girl
You shot into my life in May
In an instant things developed
Colour appeared from the grey

You are my half-time team talk
You spur me on to better things
Inspirational and determined
I'll play till the fat lady sings

You are my favourite flower
You seem to bloom for me
Like a mysterious orchid
With sweet floral harmony

You are my Taj Mahal
You are a wonder of today
A perfect human structure
To take my breath away

You are my bird of paradise
You are my wildest dream
In a nature documentary
You're my favourite scene

Colin Halsall, Wigan, Greater Manchester

FOR MUM

You were always there
When I needed you
You always saw me through
In good times
And in bad times
I could always count on you
You saw me
Through my darkest days
You cheered me
Through the good
You always did
Everything for me
As only a mother could

Alison Worsley, Stockport, Greater Manchester

ONE MOMENT IN TIME

I saw him coming along my way
This is it I thought at last
My heart was pounding like a drum
So hard and very fast
One moment in time he glanced my way
His eyes were blue and soft
His hair was like the summer hay
Blonde with a little wave on top
As he passed me by he gave a smile
Hello he spoke oh so very sweet
Madame may I take you to the ball tonight
And dance you off your feet
And now we are happily married
My blonde blue eyed young man and me
We've got three lovely babies
And lots of memories

Rosaleen Dean, Stockport, Greater Manchester

AUNTIE BETTY

Whenever I think of my childhood
My thoughts turn to you, Auntie Bet.
Fond memories fill me with pleasure
Of times I'll never forget.

My mum would pack my belongings
In a brown and battered suitcase
To be by the sea with my cousins
To put colour back in my face.

We played all day in those war years
With never a tear or care
Lived on chips and ice-cream
And anything else you could spare.

Read comics, wrote plays combed the beach
Only one thing the day to spoil.
When standing in line at bedtime
You doled out the cod liver oil.

You've now reached your ninetieth birthday
Surrounded by love and respect
Thanks for a wonderful childhood
I love you so much, Auntie Bet.

Jean Fogo, Failsworth, Greater Manchester

UNTITLED

My vanity an empty shell
Washed and battered by the sea
Now I'm unsure, can this be hell?
You're gone from me with no farewell
And like a shell upon the sand
I vacant and forgotten stand
Waiting for the barbarous sea
To vanquish and devour me

Joan Salisbury, Stockport, Greater Manchester

NORTH WALES MEMORIES

Have you ever spent a weekend in Llandudno,
Or perhaps you've had a week in Rhos-on-Sea?
You may have walked along the coast to Abergele
And back to Colwyn Bay in time for tea.

I expect you've been across the bridge to Anglesey
And then motored on a bit to Benllech Bay.
Have you ever holidayed in sweet Beaumaris
Or been to old Rhosneigr for the day?

I once spent half the night on Cader Idris,
To see the sun rise early in the morn,
And then trekked up to Snowdon on a lovely summer's day
And stayed amongst the hills until the next day's dawn.

So, if you have such memories to dream of,
Just send old friends a card to reminisce,
And sign it with your love and great affection,
And seal it with a very special kiss.

Shirley C Daniels, Stockport, Greater Manchester

THE CHURCH GATES

Now blue and as good as new
Fencing off our rhubarb patch.
They were found lying in the grass.
There at the back of the church
They did sit. The path was widened
They would no longer fit.

What could they tell us and recall,
The weddings and the funerals
In sunshine and in snowfall.
The folks who trod the path
Wearing their best outfits
Or humble bonnet and shawl.

A meeting place for neighbours,
A treasured building once,
But gone its raison d'etre.
No longer accepting its dogma
Folks keep their ethics still.
And the Church stands
Like a beacon on a hill.

Doris Thomson, Middleton, Greater Manchester

SO CLOSE

We are apart
But as one
We are separate entities
Yet entirely belong
To one another
And now, so close
As we sleep
We've seen the last of grief

Adrian Johnson, Wigan, Greater Manchester

FAILSWORTH GHOSTS

When melancholy drizzle shrouds the water
And the street lighting is switched on before tea.
Then do the ghostly legions' footsteps falter
With their pad and tap and whispering to me?
Steady marching through the marshes
Stepping one behind the other.

Lurking speed humps in Roman Road
They don't see.

As evening sun ebbs over the city
And jaded homeward bound commuters retire.
Stagecoach pitching and brigand without pity
Desperate plunder near the toll bar does conspire.
Between the perilous hedges
On the fringes of the heathland.

Happy eaters in McDonalds
He doesn't see.

Heather Ferrier, Failsworth, Greater Manchester

FIRST LOVE

Each is different and unique,
Some stand times test,
Others are the template for those that follow
And deny the chance for true happiness,
Or find once more that first perfection
For a few their perfection is beyond realities reach,
And they are doomed to a endless search
Along the road of broken love.

Matthew Taylor, Oldham, Greater Manchester

A SPECIAL GUY

I was very young when I met him
He was so handsome with lovely brown eyes
I was too young to know what love really was
But I knew he was a special guy

A few years on I married him
This special guy of mine
And through all our ups and downs in life
He remains my special guy

We've had a lot of laughs along the way
And a few bad times too
But my special guy was always there
Always knowing the right thing to do

We have two sons who are now grown men
With lives to live of their own
I know to them he's a special guy
The main man and the anchor of our home

Vi Binns, Cheadle, Greater Manchester

THE WHITE FEATHER

There was an angel on my doorstep.
She left a feather of snowy white.
I know the angel on my doorstep
Is watching over me each night.
For when I'm feeling sad and lonesome,
And I am oh, so very blue.
I think of the angel on my doorstep
Who left a message there from you.
It tells me never feel downhearted,
Just take inspiration from the start,
And do the things I want to do
That I feel deep within my heart.
So I sit and write with vengeance.
Thoughts come tumbling from my head.
I sometimes wish I had been an artist
And painted scenery instead.
So I try within my poems
To paint a picture, just for you
Then the angel on my doorstep
Will have made my dreams come true.

Lilian Hart, Bolton, Greater Manchester

MY UNDYING LOVE

My undying love is all I can give
I'll give it to you as long as I live
Holding my hand as we walk down the pier
I'll give all my heart to you my dear
Kissing and cuddling in the dead of night
I'll let my emotions go and hold you tight
Embracing my charms with all my heart
I'll love you forever and never depart

Graham Scotson, Bury, Greater Manchester

SUPERMARKET SHOPPING

For forty years, his wife has shopped
And done it quite superbly.
She scrimped and saved and made ends meet
And waited on him, hands and feet.

But now retired, he comes along
To show her where she's going wrong.
Around the aisles he looks for stuff
And tells her when she has enough.

He floats just like a butterfly
Deciding what he'd like to buy
And while he ponders which to do
The other people can't get through.

I always shopped in half an hour
But now it takes me double.
If only wives would shop alone
I wouldn't have this trouble.

Maureen Harrison Riley, Norden, Greater Manchester

THEN YOU SMILED

Soon the sun warmed the daytime
Saw the water flowing free
Soon your eyes told me that you were glad
Of the company.

Sang a song of sky and sunlight
Felt the need to rest awhile
Far away a voice was calling me
Then you smiled.

Then from time to time you'd leave me
Picking flowers like a child
And you held my hand to lead me home
Then you smiled

Smiling sweetly turning me
To face the sun
Smiling all the time to tell me
I'm the one
You love

Frances Rochelle Barrie, Prestwich, Greater Manchester

LIMIT

Dictionary definition: "the unspeakable extreme of
endurability"
Chains on my feet, I cannot meet you.
Lips sealed against my tongue.
My heart chaffs against restriction,
Because you say I must not come.

Alice J Campbell, Greater Manchester

TOFFEE APPLES

Look at that toffee apple
It's covering half your face
Bulging eyes are just appearing
You really look a case.

Whatever in life you want to try
We'll buy it just for you
But if it's a toffee apple
Can we get sticky too?

Now your nose has got afast
That red sticky apple has stuck so fast
We'll have to get you to the sink
Oh, look your teeth have turned all pink.

We've got it off at last you're free
But two loose teeth have gone we see
How cute and beautiful you still look
They may be back for Christmas with luck.

Sylvia Lee-Wild, Rochdale, Greater Manchester

TIME

We met and we
Said our hellos.
She's the love of your life,
We're informed and,
That's the way the wind blows.
You both sat together,
Upon the settee and,
All that I saw,
Holding hands was,
Your dad and me.
Soon you will be parents,
Have your own little gem,
Then you'll become us and,
As for your grandparents,
Well, we'll become them.
The world keeps on turning,
The clock it goes round,
In each others shoes,
Sooner or later,
Most will be found.

Sheila Valerie Baldwin, Wigan, Greater Manchester

PRECOGNITION

She gazed upon the infinite blue
Fearful of its artifice,
Espied the trapdoor sky possesses,
For little girls to fall into.

Pamela Igoe Hall, Littleborough, Greater Manchester

GONE BUT NOT FORGOTTEN

Always there for you whenever you need me
Forever in my mind you will always be
Forever in your heart I will always be there
Even when I am gone memories won't be a blur
Chosen times I'm sure you will remember
Talking all night those cold nights in December
I will never forget those special days
Only you will remember my special ways
Never will you forget the good times we shared
Affectionately you showed me how much you cared
Today you must start your life again
Even though you are going through so much pain
Lonely nights will come and slowly go
You'll find someone else that much I know
You are not to sit around feeling so sad
Or when you meet someone else start to feel bad
Under no circumstances will you forget how we began
Remember to enjoy your life as much as you can
Stay strong because you will always be my special man.

Kelly Morgan, Swinton, Greater Manchester

THE SEA WITHIN ME

To the sea I say with warm affection, what a wondrous
thing you are! Earth's beautiful blue mantle, swirling in
frolicking winds delicately scented by many lands.
In your depths lie mystic coral forests, remote as distant
moons, where silvery fish dart over long-lost gold coins,
man's tiny mirrors, reflecting nature's glory. You embrace
frozen islands, where sunlit ice crystals blaze in the
enchanted fire of intense cold, enfolding themselves
in multicoloured beauty. You are nocturnal tropical waters,
aglow with phosphorescent fire, and spangled with exotic
jellyfish, living chandeliers with dimmed lights, gently
treading the caressing waters of the twilit deep.
You flourish mountainous waves, avalanches of molten
snow,
that maybe started in Alps or Himalayas and
worked their passage into warmer waters. You are
power and gentleness in a perfect eternal balance.
You were indeed, o sea, a fitting place for life's
first dawn, and I, as one of your grateful
descendants, salute you!

Stuart McEwen, Denton, Greater Manchester

Stuart McEwen said: "I am a retired analytical chemist,
mainly engaged in outdoor activities, but also interested in
two art forms - painting (I display my work in local exhibi-
tions) and writing. I have written two plays which have
been performed on the amateur stage, but most of my writ-
ing has been confined to scientific papers. I have, however,
written a few poems and several hymns as a hobby. I am a
member of the Society of Authors."

A GIRL IN SUDDEN SUNLIGHT

Suddenly it entered through the window,
Inside the room the light of the bright sun,
Startled she turned to see its warming glow
Upon the woven pattern of her gown.

Until this moment day had lain in mist,
The sky of stone with intermittent rain,
When to her almost unbelief were cast
The rays of this most brightening sunborn sheen.

Wakeful she saw it blaze the book-shelf glass
And in a wounding escalate the wall,
Where like a wind there blew a restlessness
Which was to take possession of her soul.

It seemed that in the light she heard her name,
That there afar she saw new lands unfold,
While now as if to dance she stood in flame,
In summoning glow as of another world.

Danny Milne, Rochdale, Greater Manchester

Danny Milne said: "Writing poetry is a need for me rather than a hobby. It is an attempt to capture aspects of the human condition in its various moods. It first began when reading Shakespeare's sonnets and conditions of the human heart and mind. Later I read translations of European and Asian poetry of which their beauty on reading made my hair stand on end. Poetry for me is about expression and craftsmanship. It is a dare into the fire of emotions. It comes at a certain unpredictable moment like the moment of a butterfly before it flies away."

A GIRL LIKE YOU

When you speak to me I know
I will always love you so
The way you love, the way you talk
The way you hold me as we walk
I know that I, I have nothing
But my love to offer you
But you know every day it's brand new
I hope that one day we will marry
And my child you will carry
That will sure be like heaven to me
But till then I will hope
I may mope but I will cope
Because a girl like you loves me.

David Keevil, Oldham, Greater Manchester

Born in Oldham **David Keevil** has interests including collecting Elvis Presley records and walking his dog. "I started penning verses when I wrote a song to cheer my wife up when she was ill," he explained. "My work is influenced by my life and family and I would like to be remembered as someone who brought a little joy to the people he met." Aged 39, David works as a blending line supervisor and has an ambition to get one of his songs published. He is married to Elaine and they have children Trina, Lisa, Clair and Kevin. "I have written three novels, many songs and a large number of poems," he added.

MY BEST FRIEND

I'd just like to tell you about my dear friend
So if you have a spare minute to spend
I'd like you to know all the nice things about
This considerate person I can't be without
Who listens to all of my sadness and woes
Considers my feelings with kindness that shows
Who can be relied on to be there each day
To share each experience life sends our way
We share all our problems and joys when we need
There's no better person to be with indeed
This person is one of a most special few
I just had to mention, my best friend is you.

Joan M Jones, Prestwich, Greater Manchester

LET'S LIVE TOGETHER

I have been with you for years now
Which prompts a cause for thought
About how we live together
Before all comes to naught
And if you see things my way
And I strongly suggest you should
Then we will be fit for years to come
Which can only be to the good
I will rise with you in the morning
I will lie down with you at night
I will always be there strong for you
If you always treat me right
I will be with you through good and bad
As I have been from the start
I will be with you forever
Affectionately yours, ba-boom, ba-boom, your heart.

Ron Walls, Darwen, Lancashire

SUMMER MEMORIES

The warm summer raindrops that kiss your face are -
My joyful tears.

The soft soothing sigh of the gentle breeze is -
My whisper in your ear.

The pure, sweet scent of your favourite rose is -
The perfume I now wear.

The pretty butterfly you often see is -
A sign that I am here.

The first tasty tang of that wild blueberry is -
A taste we used to share.

But when summer memories fade with time,
I'll still hold you in my care - forever.

Dorothy M Ellis, Garstang, Lancashire

FRIENDS

To all my friends I write with thanks
For the time in my life when they are here
The young and older ones who share
The rough and the smooth, the bad and the good
My love for all things splendid and beautiful

Through the eyes of a child, simple things
The bursting of a flower, grown from seed
The butterflies and birds on the wing
The ladybird and bee with its velvet body touching
The blossoms to take pollen from one to the other.

The rabbits, squirrels, the lambs in the fields
Bring happiness, love and joy to every girl and boy
So as we grow we remember the days gone by
When we were young my friends and I
And with affection I can still you all, why?

Margaret Mohyla, Preston, Lancashire

MEET THE CLASS

I was asked to write of the creative writing class,
So would you like to meet us?
We are sometimes factual,
We are always cheerful,
We are creative
We are productive
Often imaginative, we are ingenious
We are inspired, producing is fertile
We are always original
The creative writing class,
Yes that is us.

Susan Atkinson, Colne, Lancashire

*Dedicated to the tutors of "Explore your potential" course at
Nelson and Colne College. Thankyou for your time and effort.*

SONNET TO SPRING

This is the season I adore,
And do revere it more and more;
A song thrush now began to sing,
In celebration of the spring;
I pondered then, just like the spring,
What's the best of anything?
The wonder of beginning.
These days of ever-growing light
Imbue me with unique delight;
I mused if then we only might
Rein in this season's headlong flight;
But we, like seasons, ebb and flow;
People come into our lives and go;
Shall it be forever so?

Geoffrey W Lever, Preston, Lancashire

EXPRESSIONS OF LOVE

It was an old lace edged greeting card
Tucked within a page of a book, I bought
The lovely words wrote be a poetic bard
With hearts and roses in true style caught

My fingers glided gently across the shapes
The brightly embossed emblems came alive
It was a moment lost in time as if it escapes
Into a mystery in the minds eye to contrive

A little hidden piece, a treasure of yesteryear
Charming and sweet in an expression of love
A feeling of the innocence of time, so very dear
Of a perfect sincere verse made in heaven above

Just a simple message of love that silently pours
From the soul and signed "Affectionately Yours."

Dawn Prestwich, Lytham St Annes, Lancashire

MY LOVE

I don't often say I love you,
For you know it's not my way,
But I hope I can convince you,
In what I have to say.
you are the sunshine in my life,
Without you, how could I live,
And if I had to save you,
My life I'd gladly give.

There is nothing in this whole wide world
That means more to me,
For you are all I want.
And that will always be.

So though I don't say it often,
The love I have for you,
I thank God for the joy you bring,
And for our happiness to.

Ruth Zardecki, Darwen,Lancashire

MY LOVE

Should I ignore the sparkle of the stream?
Or awaken from sleep so I cannot dream.
My pleasure in smelling the scent of the flowers,
Or wandering the countryside in dawns early hours.
I see the beauty around me through my tears,
And think of the pleasures we shared
Through the years.
You cannot see now these lovely things,
A kiss goodbye, then you opened your wings.

Iris Tennent, Earby, Lancashire

SOMEDAY

I hear you call
Like a whisper in my ear
So far away
A person I'm yet to meet
Somewhere else
Waiting for me
I hear you call
Like a gentle breeze
From far away shores
Always there
In some far away place
Waiting for our paths to cross
Someday down the line
I hear you call
A friend, a lover
Waiting to meet unexpectedly
In some far off day

Oliver Waterer, Fleetwood, Lancashire

OUR KIND OF LOVE

To sit beside you, oh so close
I long to kiss your face,
But kisses lead to other things
And sometimes, to disgrace.

The closeness is so challenging
I want to merge with you,
I love you, love your loving eyes
And no one else will do.

To sit beside you, oh so close
I want for nothing more,
Tis you and you alone my dear,
That I really do adore.

We do not even need to speak
Just breathe each others breath,
Yes, this will really do for me
Until my hour of death.

Irene Charlton, Clitheroe, Lancashire

LEST WE FORGET

Imagine waking up one day to horror beyond all creed
Where grief so cruel became the fuel
For one man's evil deed.
Camps of death did sap the breath of untold sinless souls
As one by one and naked stood
They closed those chamber doors.
Aushwitz, Dachau name but two where millions breathed
their last
But we should not forget the truth
Of how this came to pass.
With unexpected ease one man did bring about this hell
And in respect for those who died
Their story we must tell.
Many say what's done is done. Forget it. Live for now;
Yet look how easy it came about
Those death camps at Dachau.
Should history repeat itself, I leave you all with this;
Just pray that there's a place for you
On Mr Schindler's List.

Linda Zulaica, Preston, Lancashire

IMPORTANT FOR YOU

If I have to wait forever
Then I will
For I know that I love you
From that moment I saw you
That was when I knew
I'll wait forever and I'll be by your side
For I know I love you
From that magic first moment I saw you there
I knew it
I'll wait forever if it is
I know what's important to you.

Susan Entwistle, Lancaster, Lancashire

HAYDYN

Here's a few lines about my little grandson
He is two months old and a bundle of fun
With his jet black hair and big eyes so blue
He has always got a smile for you
I love him so much, he's granny's pride and joy
I couldn't have asked for a more pleasant little boy
When he is upset the bottom lip goes all of a quiver
When he is off home to Cardiff I sit and cry a river
I miss the little chap, I've got nothing to smother
Because that's the job only given to grandmothers
A grandmother's love is different you see
A new addition is a branch on the family tree
I sit here alone waiting for the knock on the door
Then I know I can smother him in my arms once more
I will caress him all I can and give kisses galore
Because I'm your granny, I'm affectionately yours.

Jeanette Hyde, Blackpool, Lancashire

COLOURS OF LIFE

Life is about colour
A rainbow, a sunset, a stream
You'll find them all from day to day
Not just in a dream

A rainbow happens when it rains
And sunshines at one time
Red and yellow and pink and blue
Are the colours of the rhyme

Sunsets are in the evening
When the earth is quiet and still
Golden, red and orange
Magical colours over the hill

Beyond the wildest sunset
Where starlets twinkle and gleam
There is a place so far away
Where all the angels dream

Sheila M Borrowdale, Nelson, Lancashire

LOVE LETTERS

He came into my life with words of cheer
Just when I was feeling lonely and blue
The words stood out so strong and clear
I knew that every word he wrote was true

Now for me the sun shines every day
Even though dark clouds are in the sky
I push the worries of my mind away
I no longer want to hide away and cry

I read each letter over many times
I lock each word inside my happy heart
He honours me by sending loving rhymes
It is all like a dream in which I play a part

If he should leave my life tomorrow
No-one could take his words away from me
When I start to feel the pains of sorrow
I will recall again the joys he helped me see

Grace Wallace, Poulton-le-Fylde, Lancashire

THE BIRD AND I

A little bird came singing to me today
Came singing a song of cheer
I thought carry on little bird, don't go away
Your song is o, so dear.

I will throw you some crumbs if you stay
You have lifted my heart
I was feeling so down
So I went into the park.

Come near little bird I said
Do not be shy
You have a blue cap on your head
I will be sad if you should fly.

Suddenly the sky turned dark
I gave it some crumbs,
It was off with the lark
Going home to its young.

Constance M Price, Nelson, Lancashire

HORIZON

The sun goes down, the light splinters all around,
It's a beautiful sight, the heavens consume
The once needed rays so bright,
When it reaches out to all mankind
It illuminates so we can look around
To see the horizon, close the sun down.
In a dark sea of tranquillity the cosmos of stars reach on
The sun and moon guide the hands of our time
As they rise and fall, do we only see the horizon line?
No we stare in belief of something more divine.

Christopher Taylor, Poulton-le-Fylde, Lancashire

A FRIEND IN NEED

While walking the road to nowhere fast
I came upon a man, he smiled, he walked past
Stopped in my tracks, I turned to look and see
He was doing the same, he was looking at me
Are you lonely as I am, my dear friend
Yes I replied, not sure how it would all end
Lets sit a while, eat and have a chat
He lay out a feast on an open mat
I smelt the flowers and the beautiful rye grass
I knew I was glad I had not walked past
Oh this lovely man, his meal he did share
No one had been kind to me, he felt my despair
The meal it was over, the sun shone on us both
Giving life's light and plenty of warmth
Then he did leave me, with great affection
As he walked away, he had been true perfection

Dorothy Greenall, Heysham, Lancashire

TRUE FRIENDS

We make many friends in a lifetime
As we travel along life's way
Some friendships are fleeting and some not so true
Just a few go on with us all the way

Sometimes in our lives we can all get hurt
If a good friend lets us down
When we feel we've been used it makes us so sad
And our smile gives way to a frown

But the friends that stick by us through thick and thin
Through the good times and the bad
These are the friends that make life worthwhile
And to have them makes us all feel so glad

The true friends are the ones who have lasted the course
And to you they would give their last dime
These are the friends we must cherish
That have stood the test of time

James Wright Ashcroft, Clayton-le-Dale, Lancashire

WHAT MEMORY

My mind is blank I can't remember
Is it December?
No it's January
Are you in a hurry?
Not to worry
Cause I can't remember
Have you got a date?
Are you running late?
Not to worry
Cause I can't remember
Is it morning?
Is it night?
If in doubt just look out
But not to worry
Cause I can't remember
Is it important?
Yes write it down
But I forgot to check
But not to worry
Cause I can't remember

Karen Pickup, Accrington, Lancashire

LOVE AT FIRST SIGHT

The moment I saw you
I loved you
The moment we touched
You were mine

I had to have you
At all costs
The price was going to be high

I certainly thought you
Were worth it
Why did I hesitate?
Quick move before
I lose you, it could be far too late

I put my hand in my pocket
To feel what lay there
Just enough to have you
The eighteenth century jug
At the fair

Margaret Fairhurst, Up Holland, Lancashire

MOTHER

I sit, and watch you looking,
but unlike me, you cannot see.
I feel the sorrow you are living,
because pain, won't let you be.
At times, when I hold you close,
and feel your ageing hands,
The frustration of living a limited life,
I try to understand.
My words, they paint you pictures,
as the days ahead, unfold.
You live your life, through the seasons,
trying to see the things you are told.
I long to take the walks, with you,
we shared, when I was young.
Kicking through autumn's leafy gown,
Life back then, was fun.
Through your lonely life in darkness,
your love has shone on through.
Because, as you keep on telling me,
That's what mothers do.

Tarni Procter, Morecambe, Lancashire

PENSIVE THOUGHTS

"Eureka" I've found a cleaner, a person
Who will attend to jobs I cannot do
Yes, I know the years have rolled on
I most certainly don't feel blue
For within this soul and heart of mine
I'm young, full of interesting chat
Not gossip that can cross the line
Making one feel haughty like a cat
Who has just lapped up a dish of cream
Never even caring who it scratches
Smugness is in residence reigning supreme
When teasing the mouse it playfully catches
Now he is taking stock of me and mine
Proudly surveying the scene ready to pounce
Knowing and showing he is in charge feeling fine
Ready to draw blood, flaunt and flounce
A cat's prerogative for owners are pawns
To their whims, being cast aside whenever
His eyes become slits he stretches and yawns
Good night to you and you, affectionately yours, forever.

Beryl Hall, Blackburn, Lancashire

THE SUPREME GIFT

If tomorrow I should die,
I'd ask you not to rue,
If I'd not lived upon this earth,
Then neither too, would you.

This gift I gladly give to you,
As I know that you will be,
A shining light where there is dark,
An ambassador for me.

Eric Dodgson, Lancaster, Lancashire

A NEED FOR PRAYER

I loved you because I needed you
A lost soul in the dark, I prayed for guidance
Then you came my way, I thank you.

I loved you because I loved you
In awe, my prayer had been answered,
Blindly I hung on each word, each deed, in need.

I loved you , I saw the truth
And slowly I backed away,
I felt the strength inside me, the strength to be free.

I love you but I feel sorry for you,
A lost soul in your darkness of life,
Praying for guidance.

I pray for you too.

Estelle Blackman, Lytham St Annes, Lancashire

A SPECIAL OCCASION

The war long over with peace enjoyed
Those days I remember upon the land
That old pork pie upon the crown
With jodhpurs wet and mucky

Affectionately yours, wrote to my beau abroad
Who fought in the heat of the desert
Yet so many letters sadly that didn't arrive
Though luckily we both survived

Now of course a century's past
With my family count of twenty
My children's, children's, children
A little boy upon last count
Great grandson, sweet and bonny

I lost my desert rat four years ago
Though I've still got his letters with ribbon tied
And I know in my heart he'll always be near
Will you see your new grandson just lately born?
Of course he'll be there and in my prayers
To celebrate our families special occasion

Elizabeth Saynor, Great Harwood, Lancashire

MEMORIES

How time passes, seems like yesterday
My children were going out to play,
Out and about with friends to meet,
Safe and secure around the street,
Just yesterday.

But now they're adults: Fully grown
With different lifestyles of their own,
Meals at the pub with colleague or friend
Phone conversations that never end
That's life today.

So what of tomorrow? Maybe then
They'll wish their childhoods back again.
Closer ties with family,
Lots of time for you and me
Or was that yesterday?

And yet I know on Mother's Day
They will be calling round to say:
"We love you, Mum" , I know that's true
It matters not what else they do,
My love will last forever.

Monica Cole, Cleveleys, Lancashire

SEALED WITH A LOVING KISS

First love, is like no other, when
The heart quickens, beating,fluttering,
Inside like the wings of a thousand
Butterflies trying to escape.

Love letters easier to write down
The feelings of love you share
But are too shy to express
Openly, yet feel so deeply.

The trusting when circumstances part you
For a while, though letters are still
Written and received each affectionately coded
S.W.A.L.K, sealed with a loving kiss.
The heartbreak when the last letter begins
Dear K, and ends D. It is over.
The aftermath when nothing can console you
And your dreams and emotions are shattered.

Slowly you survive and go through the
Motions of living, but the tears have
Drowned all the butterflies, so a new love
Can never quite compare with the first.

Vera Entwistle, Bolton, Greater Manchester

OH MY DEAREST ONE

Oh, dear Nell, no-one could tell,
How much I miss your smile
Along with your sweet lips,
And your caressing finger tips,
Without you it will feel like hell.

You said that I should not cry,
When you said your last goodbye.
You said, "you'll find another woman to love,"
But there'll never be another, friend or lover
My hearts breaking and now I know why.

These fifty-two years have soon flown by,
My dearest, my darling, my love.
I have memories to share,
And plenty to spare,
Now you go, and it's my turn to cry.

What's done is done, the cancer has won,
What else could be done to help you stay?
With all the prayers I have said,
As you've lain ill in that bed,
Now the Angels will have their way.

David Anderson, Hoghton, Lancashire

MY TEDDY BEAR

My teddy bear, my confidante, my friend
Abandoned now, you sit upon your shelf
And watch me through the night
Once you shared my bed
Close cuddled, warm and soft,
We shared the dreams.

Worn now with time long passed
Dim eyes that once were bright
Red jacket faded with the light
Of many years of sun and life.

Yet still you hold a special place
We've grown together through our age
I know you're always there for me
When friend I need and so you be.
I tell you all my pain and woes
You comfort me and hold me close.

So though you sit upon your shelf
As years go by, become the past
Yet still you are my teddy bear,
My faithful confidante, my loyal friend.

Jean Emmett, Accrington, Lancashire

INEFFABLE

The wholeness of the sky,
its blessings of pure light,
Two simple eyes bring, and well with tears,
bow, humble below it;
at the awesome power of sight.

Silence, the sound of peace,
Two abused ears, sings quiet the song
of eternal time and the passing of the seconds,
Tick. A resounding note, echoed in birdsong
each breath of wind through grass blades.

The world about you,
immensity mirrored in every minutiae,
steals the breath of all those who dare,
to look upon the sea, the infinite horizon,
the majesty of mountains blinds unguarded eyes.

Essence of love, so filling a heart,
beyond its brink, a power so strong,
so as to crush it beneath its weight
kneel beneath the trees and weep
for love beyond expression.

Rebekah Foulkes, Preston, Lancashire

OUR WORLD OF MAKE-BELIEVE

How we rode on santa's sleigh
in our own little world of pretend.
I made up stories of fairy tales
which we never thought would all end.

Make believe and puppet shows
our days so full of fun.
We let no one in, this world was ours
not even included our mum.

Together we played so many games
our hearts were like as one.
The happiness we felt so precious but ...
those years just didn't last long.

Growing up we could not avoid
that world of ours it faded.
No more make believe in our lives
as from those early years we waded.

Brothers and sisters gradually part
yet, that magical world we treasure,
and still so close despite the miles
our childhood bond will last forever.

Clifford Chambers, Blackpool, Lancashire

THE PHOTOGRAPH

Thumbprinted gloss four by six
With corners bent and frayed
Lined up were a motley mix
Of people stiff and staid

Formerly black, now nearly brown
The snapshot was concealed
Inside an envelope stuck down
And from which the stamp had peeled

A serious girl stood at the rear
With a cross above her head
I'm sorry this is not too clear
But this is me dear Ted

Do take care the letter said
And write to me when you can
I pray for you each night in bed
Because you know you are my man

I've loved you so for many years
How I wish this war would end
The marks on this snapshot are my tears
'Cause you're not home with me, dear friend

Eric Irwin, Thornton-In-Cleveleys, Lancashire

NITS

I'm sorry to tell you
But your daughter has fleas
We've all seen them crawling
Through her hair to her knees

We really can't blame you
You're not privileged we know
But would you mind standing
More than a stones throw

A sign could be useful
And perhaps a small bell
Just to remind us
And advise others as well

There's a very nice alcove
It's just over there
Away from us mothers
Who really do care

And so let us finish
Here's a gift, a nit tool
With love and affection
Signed, the whole school

Rachel Butterworth, Burnley, Lancashire

NATALIE'S FOURTH BIRTHDAY

Mummy taught me how to write
The numbers one, two, three
What do those numbers mean
To a dear little girl like me
They tell me I have lived those years
And each one shows I've grown
But every one is secret
And all my very own
But what about this day of mine
The postman at the door
Leaving envelopes for me
'Cos guess what? I am four
Isn't that a lovely age
For me, for Natalie
I hope we get some callers
With presents just for me
Daddy will be oh, so pleased
My birthdays come at last
And Mummy will agree with him
That time has flown so fast
Daddy still enjoys himself
Especially playing pool
And Mummy must be thinking
Next year I'll go to school

Joseph Alston, Lancaster, Lancashire

THE EARTH AND THE FIRE

The earth is scorched by the raging fire,
Live flames burning, higher and higher,
Blistering the grass, tormenting the trees,
Taking no prisoners, no birds, no bees.

This death light, zapping everything in its way,
A terrifying delight burns night and day,
Out of control but precisely so it seems,
Nothing escapes this violence and direct sunbeams.

Penetrative, bursting through all living things,
A hostility rampage is what this fire brings.

Peace at last, the inferno is no more,
But after the mayhem, earth's won this war,
She's a wicked nature for she has very deep roots,
The mother earth gives birth, to newly sprung shoots.

After a while her magic spreads to buds,
As quickly as that there's a whole new type of woods,
It seems nothing can stop this fast growing spree,
Jesus nor Mohammad, nor you, nor me.

God and the elements are a force unmatched,
Earth forgives fire because she's only scratched.

Ben Lee Almond, Burnley, Lancashire

HOPELESSLY DEVOTED TO YOU

I will love you, 'til the hands of time stand still
'Cos, your presence gives me such a thrill.

I will love you, 'til the sun shall no longer rise
'Cos, without you I don't have dry eyes.

I will love you , 'til all the seas run dry
'Cos, without your love I will cry.

I will love you, 'til the clouds no longer form
'Cos, without your love I am forlorn.

I will love you, 'til the birds sing no more
'Cos, my love for you knows no cure.

I will love you, 'til the rain no longer falls
'Cos, for you my broken heart calls.

I will love you, 'til all the ice caps melt
'Cos, my feelings are truly heartfelt.

I will love you, 'til the world ceases to turn
'Cos, for your love I will always yearn.

I will love you, 'til the sun sets for the last time
'Cos, you will then be eternally mine.

Elsie Ryan, Skelmersdale, Lancashire

JUST A LITTLE BIT

You were given many talents
On the day that you were born
Eyes that twinkle in a smiling face
Capable of functioning at dawn
Both health and personality
Will help you through this life
Sense of humour and a loving heart
Support by husband friend and wife
Diplomacy and charm essential
For homemaker washer up and cook
But the thing that you need most of all
Is just a little bit of lady luck

Winifred Smith, Colne, Lancashire

AN ON-GOING JOKE

I play my music, you complain
Then howl the lyrics like an opera singer
A great contradictor, still you say you're not
People who rang got your telephone catchphrase
"Hello Tolond" - now a long running family joke
Sunday's singing, "Songs of Praise" as you finish off the
spuds
My middle aged father, wincing like a child
Accustomed to your behaviour, still he runs away
Your high pitched scream bellows over Royden, "Billy, Billy,
Billy"
On early mornings, in those odd looking walking boots
And sometimes I dread ringing your house
In case I'm not greeted with the telephone catchphrase
"Hello Tolond" cannot go on forever
But a long running family joke can.

Emma-Jayne Tolond, Birkenhead, Merseyside

BEAUTY

There is something of lingering beauty
In the shelved photograph album
Smiling faces on visits to family and friends
Memorable moments shared in another age and time

Searching for a picture of a lovely garden
To write an article or a poem
A relatives face looks back vividly at you
And the light mood is changed to sadness
As that day lived out in another life
Revives memory of pastimes

Those letters once written so correctly
To an aunt who knitted a Christmas gift
Ending with affectionately yours
The thank you note is now given a lift
With a modern day snap
That tells so much without a written word

Freda Grieve, Formby, Merseyside

PEBBLE

Stone so smooth
Weathered by force

You were there
Before me desolate
On the sand of time
You were never mine

I place you back to
Take the weight

Becoming once more
Of time and tide
Never to be mine

Marj Kurthausen, West Kirby, Merseyside

FROM ME TO YOU

There's a poem for every occasion from "I love you" to
"Sorry I broke your heart."
A poem is a song without music, which you can sing with a
little imagination,
You can memorise it in the dark.

A poem is a personal message to someone racked with
pain.
Or sorrow from the death of a loved one.
Words of compassion can get you on your feet again.

A poem can heal the wounds of every day living.
Kind words can say "hello" or "goodbye" with a smile.
We can appreciate each day as a gift, and walk another
mile.

Janet Forster-Foote, St Helens, Merseyside

JUST A CALL AWAY

You have done the things I never have
You have pulled off the mightiest tasks
I am in so much admiration for you
But I am jealous of you behind my many masks

That brother-sister bond is so very strong
I am the heavyweight, but so shy - yet angry
You are so headstrong, so confident
You are also the beauty - I am the beast

You know how much I am still always here
Just a call away to be by your side
We defend each other so very much
If I were a lion, I'd be the head of the pride

Never stop achieving your dreams
I was always the let down
Be forever happy now that you're a mum
Keep on smiling, never showing a frown

Anthony Clements, Wallasey, Merseyside

SWEET NELL

Nell you are a lady fair
Whose manner is beyond compare
A film star you should have been
With your looks fit for a queen
Your wonderful figure is always dressed
In clothing that is only the best
You are a vision to behold
So forgive my staring which is bold
My heart also misses a beat
Whenever I see you on the street
To see you is a wonderful sight
Whether it's morning, noon or night
So please sweet Nell, join me soon
During spring's romantic moon

Thomas McCabe, Liverpool, Merseyside

A DAUGHTER REMEMBERS

In the corner of our house stood an old piano,
Most nights years ago
My mam used to play all the songs of the day
From honky-tonk to rock and roll and ballads
She could make the piano speak

In the corner of the house years ago
Stood an old piano the tunes I hear still
On the stool sat my mam
Her magic fingers flying over the keys
In days gone by in the local
A crowd would gather to hear her play
All the songs of the day
Now I hope she is in heaven
Playing to her heart's content

Frances Brothers, Speke, Merseyside

123

DEAR ISABELLA

Dear Isabella, my sister, my muse
I write in great sorrow to tell of our news,
mother is,
well, mother is as expected,
distraught.
Dear Isabella, dear comforter, aid and support,
I beseech you, I need you, be by my side,
with me and our mama, do abide.
Dear Isabella, dear sister, my right hand.
Our father, well father, so beguiling,
so grand.
So father, well father, so arrogant, so aloof
woke up this morning, and reaching the roof,
as Icarus kitted himself out,
feathers and string, waxed and anointed,
faced to the sun, raised up his arms,
and without any fuss, launched himself thus,
gone.
Without fuss.

Lynda Day-Bidston, Bootle, Merseyside

THE VILLAGE

Walking down the village street and feeling all at home
The shops, the cars, the children playing, nobody alone
The trees that grow in pavements, the lovely sandstone walls
The butchers, bakers, saddle-makers, church and old church hall
I love the polished brass nameplates of lawyers, near the bank
Those most official letters, showing all their pomp and rank
And I remember years before when I was so beguiled
When mother shopping these same shops, the sweets, the greedy child
The Royal Oak with ancient windows, pubby smells within
Where tired men, at end of day, would meet for beers and chin
I loved it then, I love it now, my village and my kin
And as I walk my grandsons here, I know they'll carry on
The peace that is my village life is wealth beyond compare
A wealth that can't diminish as it steadily is shared

John Michael Corfe, West Kirby, Merseyside

WHY I LOVE HER SO

Beautiful as any flower
Delicate as the finest china
Yet as strong as the mighty oak
Enchanting as witchcraft
As innocent as a lamb
As constant as mother nature
Yet as free and wild as the wind
Bright as any star
Volatile as fire
Serene as an angel
As beautifully imperfect as the Mona Lisa
So human
That is why I love her so

Dave Lunn, Wallasey, Merseyside

IN TIME

"They" say that time's the healer and to a point I would
agree,
But how to deal with loneliness when you're not here with
me.
No one to share a thought with or exchange a loving smile,
Or touch my hand, or give a hug, and make it all worth-
while.
All the years we shared together, the good times and the
sad,
Because we were together nothing seemed so bad.
Everything seemed easier with two of us to share,
Also that much happier with two of us to care.
But we cannot turn the clock back,
Just carry on each day and know we're close,
In spirit, no matter what "they" say.

Martha Birch, Upton, Merseyside

SITTING ON A BENCH ON THE PROM

Comfortable in their silence,
They sit together side by side.
Words of love spoken long ago,
Not on the tongue, but deep inside.
Both are content with life that's been,
Each others thoughts so well they know.
A love grown stronger down the years,
To golden wedding from sweet sixteen.
No holding hands or sly caress,
They don't need a lover's sign.
He'll fix her scarf - she'll pour him tea,
They're still each others Valentine.

Joan Miller, Liverpool, Merseyside

BYGONE TOYS

I once had a dolly missing one eye
All ragged and tatty and short of a shoe,
Its stuffing hung out and it lost its own cry
But its huggable friendship remained long and true.
If I were to ask you of your favourite toy
I'm sure you'd agree to remember them still,
And regardless of being a girl or a boy,
There's nought to compare with a toy's magic thrill.
Too soon do we grow with our toys left behind
And its never as though we intended to lose,
Our treasures of old that we now cannot find
Being stored up within as fond memories we muse.
Our toys have long served out duration of need
They were helpful, supportively growing-up aides,
Its good to remember their comforting deed -
Let's uphold their memory lest the magic soon fades.

Janet Morris Evans, Liverpool, Merseyside

I AM A WOMAN

I am the bringer of new life
The catalyst between love and strife
I nurture the future to its full potential
I protect and nurture those too weak to protest
I am a woman

I am the descendant of Eve
I use my wiles to please
I am the lover you want
I am the knowledgeable font
I am a woman

I can be gentle yet strong
Cunning and open
Quick to defend my hopes and my dreams
On me mankind depends
I am the keeper of knowledge
The teacher of the world
I am a woman

Kathleen Baccino, Liverpool, Merseyside

FIRST LOVE

Our eyes met but did you recognise me?
Do you remember how it used to be?
The sweet love that both of us once shared,
In the days when I believed you cared.

What happened, why did we drift apart?
It was me that you wanted at the start.
Then the phone calls stopped you went away,
After you promised that you'd always stay.

I met someone else and you did as well,
Of our time together I didn't tell.
It was so special I'm glad that we met,
And as long as I live I'll not regret.

That you were my first love but not my last,
All that we had is now well in the past.
But I'll not forget you and I can see,
By your secret smile you won't forget me.

Ann Blair, Prenton, Merseyside

THE GOOD OLD DAYS

When we look back and times were hard
We even had a privy in our back yard
The bathtub hung on a nail in the wall
Get your clothes off my mother would call
There would be fights to be first in the tub
As the last one in, it would be nothing but mud
When you think about the good old days
People seem to see them through a happy haze
In the bedroom there was no TV on the shelves
We didn't even have a bed to ourself
So remember when you next look back in time
Then washing dripping on the line
It wasn't all good, it wasn't all bad
Just a bit different I'd say and a little bit sad

Catherine Chesters, Birkenhead, Merseyside

STAY WARM

Stay warm towards each other all your lives.
Give each other comfort, come what may.
That is how a deep-held love survives,
Nurtures you, whatever comes your way.

For if you have each other's loving glow
To warm your hearts in everything you do,
Whatever difficulties come and go,
That gentle radiance will see you through.

Oh, passion has its place, no doubt of that,
And romance does give life a rosy cast,
But some romantic gestures can fall flat,
The heat of passion may not always last,
While that slow burn of truly felt affection,
Will always give your lives a sure direction.

Pat Fearon, Liverpool, Merseyside

ACROSS THE GREAT DIVIDE

You were my great grandmother
And I never saw your face
Not even in the photographs
Stored in the album case.
Of course I never could have met you
For you had died before I lived
But the only photo that existed
Was of your back, your face was hid.
And that I know was for a reason
Because you were a different race
I can only just imagine
The narrowness that was your space.
For you were never talked about
Grandfather, your son never spoke of you
And when he died grandmother told me
Your race, native American was true.
Sadly dad always denied your race, and his own self
But genes and your enduring spirit have not died
And you are held in my affection and my children's
Constantly, across the great divide.

Christine Hale, Wallasey, Merseyside

WATER ON THE BRAIN

Diving under the sink, as if insane
To turn off the supply her ultimate aim
I will cure that drip, was her muffled cry
As a jet of water hit her in the eye
She grabbed the stopcock, gripping so tight
But it would not turn, filling her with fright

All the family were laughing, falling about
Get me a bucket she began to shout
Why so much water? Don't know why
Especially when my hands are still quite dry.

The deluge stopped but from where had it come
Then the penny dropped, she glared at her son
He was jumping up and down, making such a racket
Trying to hide a water-gun under his jacket

She leapt from the floor, soaked to the skin
Screaming that thing is going in the bin
But then, with a smile, and a forgiving quip
Said, oh, lets not bother about a very slow drip

Neville Davies, Eastham, Merseyside

HANDS

The silent stars go sliding by
As we set sail just you and I
Beneath a moon all silver bright
Holding hands this moonlit night
The ship sails on the ocean wide
Like a swan upon a pond doth glide.

Albert Carpenter, Rock Ferry, Merseyside

NO MORE THAN I

The sun that kisses
The blushing rose
Upon soft petalled lips,
Sips of no sweeter fare
Than I.

The sea that enfolds
In fond embrace
The gently yielding shore,
Holds no more
Than I.

All the stars that light
Up heaven's way,
Have no more to say
To you
Than I.

Albert Pearson, St Helens, Merseyside

ENCHANTMENT

You watch me sleeping in the night
hold my hand, treat me right
my sweet angel, that's what you are
I love you, you're a shining star

Life has changed since you've been here
because you cherish me and hold me dear
I've never known true love before
then you say I'm a beauty, that you can't help adore

I'm left speechless by the things you say
why, I never knew words could make me feel this way
melting into your arms, falling for your charms
unfazed by outside harms, healed with your balms

Crying with delight was new to me
now I laugh and smile, that's how it should be
lover of mine, I'd do anything for you
you make me happy, I'm no longer blue

Eve Ellen Williams, Wallasey, Merseyside

Dedicated to my shiny star, my Blunty.

THE REAL ME

I'm very fond of me,
I'm who I want to be,
I'm "one on my own,"
Not somebody's clone.
I'm very fond of me,
Because I'm who I'm meant to be.

Barbara Langton, Birkenhead, Merseyside

LIFE'S MYSTERY

Mystical and magical is the world that I perceive,
Questions do get answered in the world when you truly
believe.
Open your heart, throw your dreams to the sky,
At the end of the day we can only but try.
Synchronicity helps us to connect the dots on the
spiritual path, showing us our true life map.
Beyond coincidence, this is how we know he's there,
Whilst I travel without seeking perfection,
I consult his serenity prayer.
My world it would be a boring place, if he provided logic to
take me there.
Intuition and mysticism, a gift that is given with care.
Just live the experience, not needing to know why,
As our destinies unfold, it's written in the sky.
Life is on and running, keep living in the now,
Making love your course, affectionately yours.

Tracy Costello, Liverpool, Merseyside

RUBY WEDDING

Today we have been married
exactly forty years
and much has been accomplished
beyond our hopes and fears.

We met when we were very young
you twenty, I sixteen.
We met again the next day too.
What could these meetings mean?

We married and had children,
a girl and then a boy.
The years passed over quickly
some problems and some joy.

We had a mid-life crisis
and went our separate ways,
but again we found each other.
Some people were amazed.

We built a solid friendship
which always will endure,
and after forty years it seems
we love each other more.

Monicah Downey, Wallasey, Merseyside

DEAREST DARLING

Dearest Darling, my words are few,
In fact I cannot start.
The things that I must say to you,
Are weighing down my heart.

My promise to remain faithful,
Until death us do part,
Only remains partially intact;
I've had an affair with my heart.

How can I lose my feelings?
I guess it's simply this;
I'm hollow and I'm empty,
Even when we kiss.

I'm not in love with someone else,
The affair is in my head.
Our relationship leaves me emotionless,
I'm unhappy, I feel dead.

I respect you as a person,
I love you as a friend.
But I must leave, affectionately yours,
Our marriage is at an end.

Kim-Marie Fisher, Eastham, Merseyside

CYCLES OF THE SUN

I would forage a field of flowers,
To find the last scent of summer,
To present to you,
So you might smell the sun,
And taste the warmth
And think of me
Till the summer comes again.

Chris Terry, Prescot, Merseyside

Dedicated to Lisa Wishart, you are my everything.

MY BEST FRIEND

From the moment I saw him, he had to be mine,
Small, white and furry with a face so divine.
Could a friend be more loving, faithful and kind,
I know of no other that I'd ever find.
He gives such a welcome when I reach the door,
His body all dancing, tail brushing the floor.
I tell him my secrets, my fears and my woes,
While he listens intently, as if he just knows.
He lies down beside me when I'm in my chair,
Just sleeping and dreaming, without any care.
He is my best friend, of that I am sure,
Such wonderful company, I ask for no more.
How happy he is when we're down on the beach,
Chasing his ball and some sticks within reach.
He runs jumping at me with little wet paws,
It's as if he is saying, "I'm affectionately yours."

Hilary McShane, Hoylake, Merseyside

THE HILLS ARE ALIVE

I felt the wind upon my face
As we ran through the grass,
I heard you laugh aloud
When I fell upon my ass.

The sun drenched our hair
As we frolicked and we danced
You sang "The Sound of Music"
As I giggled whilst you pranced.

The endless sweeping fields
The green air that smells of life,
In the freedom of the open sky
We saw a magpie and his wife.

For a moment, you stopped dancing
And put your hands upon my face,
Then you kissed me oh so tender
And in the tall grass, we embraced.

I shall never forget that wonderful day
When nature overwhelmed us with pleasure,
The day you gave to me this special gift,
A memory that I do so treasure.

Juliana Bond, Birkenhead, Merseyside

JOANNE

She's got a smile
Wipe your tears
Blow your fears away
Oh those rockabye eyes
She tastes like honey and cream
In another dream
We may have been

Andrew Bruce, Liverpool, Merseyside

*Dedicated to my lovely mum, Margaret Bruce. Thank you for
a magical life mum. Your heart is bigger than an ocean.*

AS OF TODAY'S DATE

You ask me to give you my body
At times I can give you a part
You want me to love you completely
Please accept a share of my heart.
Your world revolves round my being
A weight I find hard to bear
Let others partake of your friendship
My support will always be there.
The thoughts in my head are mine
To keep or share as I choose
Don't try to control my whole spirit
Or you'll be the one who will lose.
Sir, I want to be yours faithfully
Without all the marital laws
No bonds no chains just live and let
I remain affectionately yours.

Celia Pope, Southport, Merseyside

WHEN ANGELS CALL

I've often heard it said before
A pure white feather's left on the floor,
To signify they've just passed through
And only want the best for you.

It's such an endearing way to impart
His grace and affection from His heart,
Alas, I cannot claim to know
This rare, but sweet, angelic show.

But this I can say true and sure
My angel came not so demure,
He once did live his life full on
Such strangers were we 'til he'd gone.

I wondered where he could be now
This vibrant dad who'd knit my brow,
And then he called me from above
To tell of things borne out of Love.

He spoke with such assuring voice
Of things to be, I had no choice
But to admit 'twas he I'm sure,
My Guardian Angel evermore.

Janet Morris-Evans, Liverpool, Merseyside

THE PRESENCE

When you're all alone,
And stare into the air,
Don't fear the feelings,
For it's only me there.

Relax your doubts and fears,
For you're not going mad,
For I am the lost loved one,
That once in life you had.

When I went away,
And you were looking for a sign,
You didn't have to worry,
For I was truly fine.

I'll always watch over you,
And comfort your doubts and fears,
I'll give you comfort in angelic kiss,
And wipe away your tears.

I'm not of physical presence,
But my voice is in the air,
Just remember, even though I'm gone,
I am always there.

Peter Price, Bebington, Merseyside

I WANT

I am scared. I want my mum.
I want my rug and my thumb.
I want my teddy here with me.
I want a hug on my dad's knee.
I want my friendly little dolly.
I want my biggest sister Molly.
I want my book about Piglet and Pooh.
I want my sweatshirt and hat too.
I want my furry pencil case.
I want my monkey with the funny face.
It is a very unkind rule
That I can't bring them all to school.

Wendy Black, Liverpool, Merseyside

DAMNED IN DIAMOND MINDS

Rooms gyrating turning in whispers of pain radiating upon
the
Textile tourniquet as withered soldiers vent and river in
Prehistoric chalices of rich ridden reapers sailing sound
And profound against the winter's salutations supported
and
Addressed in Cambridge chapels alive and alleviated to
Consume there the radical omniscience
Loosely chained in Dorchester Matriarchs as fire fusion
Thrusts to force the entity that shunters upon the open
Green of razor flowers all damned before the skeleton gates
And saturated against the fused fruition of gutter remis-
sions
And sun timed confessions within the shameful derision
That captures the gesticulation upon the chalice of broken
Clergy and the rapture of manic mechanics

Meleeze Zenda, St Helens, Merseyside

WHEN THE NIGHT IS BLEAK AND SILENT

When the morn is dark and cold
And birds forget to sing,
The clock upon the chest of drawers
Begins its awful ring.

You creep from 'tween the blankets
And dress without a light
Then you kiss me tenderly
And tuck me up real tight.

And it's a safe and cosy feeling
Like being a little girl,
As I slide down 'neath the bed clothes,
And 'tween the warm sheets curl.

When the night is bleak and silent
And I wake from dreams much troubled,
How good to wake and find you there,
So close besides me snuggled.

And when we lie abed late,
Just 'til the sun does shine
How sweet to wake and see your smile
And know at last you're mine.

Frankie Shepherd, Southport, Merseyside

HE, SHE AND THEY

He made me smile, we would sing,
I loved his music - none as fine,
gladness to my heart he'd bring,
a very special friend of mine.

She held my hand when I was ill,
bathed my wounds, healing pain,
guided my way with utmost skill,
in life's struggle eased the strain.

His body strength earned our wage,
when weary still had time to play,
a sportsman, teaching as a sage,
indebted I am, to this day.

For bad manners, no excuse, no foil,
she was judge, jury, dear friend too,
cook, nurse, char, - accepted toil,
a sense of humour, but wrath when due.

Skilled labourers behind life's plough,
respect and honesty lies entwined,
loving parents, that I can endow,
humble, yet proud, gems of mankind.

Harry Boyle, Southport, Merseyside

THE TEXT MESSAGE

The news was as expected,
I'm very calm you see.
I would have liked remission,
But it wasn't meant to be.
I thought of one last meeting
Before I went away.
But you would plead and argue
The reasons why I should stay.
And so this my final journey,
The bell for me now tolls.
And though the waves divide our flesh,
The stars unite our souls.

Ruth Hayes, Southport, Merseyside

THE PINK PINT

My pal Cliff drove me to Wigan
Found cheap beer, he wasn't kidding.
A neon sign said Harry's Bar.
While ago now, don't think it's still there.
Pairs there were, of mostly men.
My chasing of birds unsuccessful again.
Romantic words that I spoke,
Were all for nowt. It's a sodding bloke!
This friendly pub of meeting mates,
Where people of the same sex have dates.
I travelled here from town afar.
Stone the crows, it's a bloody gay bar!
A poofy sailor's high heels were bulled,
Clifford, bless him thought he'd pulled.
I said to Cliff: "This is just our luck,"
"We're leaving Cliff. Come on, drink up."

Philip Johnson, Rainhill, Merseyside

A CURE FOR GRANDPA

If we all sit very well
And wait our turn
And let him hug us
Even though he smells funny

If we bring him chocolates
That he isn't allowed
And eat them for him
Without making any mess

If we ask the questions
He likes to answer
Even though we already know
"How did you meet, nanny?"

If we try not to stare at the tubes sticking out
And we give him the cards we drew all by ourselves

If we pray out in the corridor
Our knees hurting on the tiles
Eyes screwed tight
With lips kissing hands

Then maybe he won't die
today

Anna Connolly, Wallasey, Merseyside

THE THISTLE

The thistle you may see as pain and beauty combined.
The thistle may draw you to either end of enemy or friend.

You can see it simply so,
As a weed, that is nettled so,
Or you can look to it,
With its lilac flowered glow.

The thistle has been classed as a weed,
But it just does its best
Quietly
And in-deed.

It comes it goes
And then year after year,
It finds needs,
So it grows.

The thistle has its thorns,
Which it proudly states
And so
And so adorns.

But does it like you and me,
Wish no more new morns?

M R Armstrong, Liverpool, Merseyside

FORBIDDEN LOVE

Worshipping you from afar
Each day I wonder where you are
If only you were here with me
How happy and content I'd be

But I can only dream and stare
I glance at you when I dare
I long to hug and feel you near
I wish for you to call me dear

A candlelit dinner just for two
Gazing eyes me and you
But thoughts of you are in my head
In reality they can't be said

A walk in the country hand in hand
Flowers bestrew our pleasant land
The sun beats down our love unites
A perfect day full of delights

Now my thoughts of you must close
Responsibilities take a hold
I must remove you from my head
An impossibility even if you were dead

Paula Burke, Liverpool, Merseyside

*Dedicated to a very special couple, my mum and dad, whom
I love dearly.*

THE PRESENT MOMENT

We looked into each other's eyes,
Knowing, not for the first time,
That it might be the last.
Intently we looked and held the gaze.

Soft hands soothed.
We listened, awaiting the words.
They came unspoken, swaddling,
Silent as warmth, close as touching.

Like ripe fruits we gathered them,
Preserving them sweet,
Seasoned and steeped in the scent,
Of the looking glass.

For me no deep searching,
I saw all that was there.
Of seventy years I knew ten well,
Could recite the sixty in stories.

And so we looked, beyond fine lashes,
And sparkling iridescence, 'til there it was,
Patent, pure and glowing,
A knowing gift of truth and love.

Lorraine Thomas, Port Sunlight, Merseyside

*Dedicated to Angela Herbert, remembered always with
enduring affection and appreciation of her inspirational
influence, her encouragement, counsel and care.*

NAN

Never a dull moment when you are about,
A compassionate lady without any doubt.
Nurturing others to conquer trouble and strife,
It's how you spend time throughout this life.
So I'll raise my glass in honour of you,
Admire and respect all the work that you do.
Sweet lady I'm proud to be part of your family tree,
This I'll say forever and confidently.
A caring and loving woman you truly are,
Ready to go the distance no matter how far.

Annette Smith, Chester, Cheshire

WEDDED BLISS

He took my tiny hand,
Upon third finger placed a band,
Vowed to love me forever,
Swore that he would leave me never.

Confetti drifted down,
Red rose petals clung to my gown,
Tears, joy and laughter gay
Filled each moment of that May day.

Tender was our love,
Surely sent from heaven above,
My heart he did fill with joy,
Yet aged nineteen was still a boy.

He bravely went to war,
Sent long love-letters by the score,
But life's just ended for me,
A telegram lies here on my knee.

Susan Williams, Crewe, Cheshire

OUR LOVE

I've been in love before
But not like this
This time feels stronger
And too good to miss

It feels so perfect
So right so nice
I feel so safe
Tucked up with you at night

You made me laugh so hard I've cried
You made me feel special, so happy so alive

I know my love for you is perfect
And nothing will ever change
In my mind we'd be together forever
And that didn't feel strange

I could never imagine being with someone new
You were for me and I was for you

I hope this never changes
I hope it will be the same
And one day we will share a home, a life
And maybe the same surname

Danielle Mellor, Warrington, Cheshire

WISHFUL FEELINGS

I wish when you tell me "I love you"
That I could say that I love you too
I like and admire you, you're my best friend
I know on you I can always depend
We've known each other for many a year
Shared fun and laughter and many a tear
But I just don't get that magic feeling
Your touch doesn't send my senses reeling
So now I'm off to distant shores
And remain as always affectionately yours

Christina Shepherd, Warrington, Cheshire

SPIDERS DIAMONDS

Glistening diamonds manyfold,
Laid on silk so fine,
For all to see but not to hold,
These stones that glint and shine.

Watched over by the fiery eyes,
That let not these stones be lost,
Victims dead, blood-dried flies,
Who've tried but paid the cost.

But O the day does have its say,
As nature bleaches bones,
To take from this web silently away,
These precious glistening stones.

For Mother Nature has the right to reclaim,
By gales, floods or blazing flame.

Jim Moss, Chester, Cheshire

THE CAT AND FIDDLE ROAD

There he rides,
Like a screaming valkyrie,
Into the burning haze of sunrise
Torso and legs,
Roughly poured into armour of leather
Badge of honour and brotherhood,
Emblazoned on his back.
A strong grip
Steers his roaring steed
Through the misty moors at speed
Up to the road,
That winds between the hills and heather.

There he rides,
Visor down,
Ribbons of hair playing tag with the wind.
He pushes on to reach
Orgasmic speed and freedom mode.
Earrings glinting for a second,
As the sunlight catches gold.
A flash of black, a whirring wheel,
The rubber smell of tyre squeal.
There he goes,
My angel lover on the cat and fiddle road.

Gay Horton, Macclesfield, Cheshire

MY COLLEAGUES, MY FRIENDS

Have you ever heard of Groundhog Day?
A repetitive edge that grinds the way
Similar surroundings, the work just the same
Growing older and playing the game
Same old story all day long
Is this belonging right or wrong?
But then a twinkle of light
A flicker of hope to save my plight
But what so good brings this to an end
My colleagues, my friends

David Jacks, Warrington, Cheshire

MY OLD PHONE BOOK

I really need a new phone book of that there is no doubt,
As every time I pick it up the pages all fall out.
It's stuffed with lots of scribbled notes, appointments to be kept,
Calling cards, old shop receipts and hotels where I've slept.
Names and numbers I don't know and some which can't be read,
And if I sifted through each page, there'd be at least six dead.
Numbers for the doctors, the dentist and a vet,
Which is quite surprising, as I've never had a pet.
I would never want for food on that you can be sure,
Just ring out for takeaways delivered to my door.
Any kind of household job in need of a quick fix,
I only have to ring for George on seven, three, four, two, six.
I have a new book sitting here but I'll just leave it be,
Because my tatty old phone book is just a part of me.

Elaine Garner, Runcorn, Cheshire

FAREWELL

Farewell my friend, who lived and now is dead.
If death is all, why not a leap to death,
for life is meaningless and has no point.
I read philosophers and saints of old
and find but doubt instead of blinding truth.
I chase the shadows of my logic heart
and split infinitives till there is naught,
naught but the chance to start out once again.
Perhaps, for those who take one leap in faith,
their heaven is life, both here and after life.
I ask you, friend, if you are there and listen,
you'll save a place for me beyond the stars.
You lived in faith. Perhaps your faith will rise,
and where I'll doubt and die in pains of death,
your faith will lift me up and give me breath.

Reginald Waywell, Warrington, Cheshire

DORSET SEE TO SEA

Towns of greying stone
Skies of scurrying clouds
Fields of flying hay
Heaths of rippling ferns
Knolls of circling trees
Brooks of dancing rain
Cliffs of scurrying clouds
Coves of lapping puddles
Beaches of sharpening pebbles
Water of flapping waves

Richard Haysom, Carlisle, Cumbria

WAITING

She was nowhere.
Sitting, frail and lost
with all her jumbled thoughts.
If only he would come,
then it would be alright again.
But he never came.
Only this other man,
who brushed her hair
softly, like he used to,
talked about things they used to do.
Perhaps he knew him?
Tried to hold her hand.
It wasn't right.
Didn't he know? Why didn't he come?

He talked and cared.
Sometimes fought back tears,
lived as best he could
within her nowhere-land.
Always there, but she never saw him.
And he loved her so.

Alison Jenner, Ulverston, Cumbria

PARTING

Every time we have to part
It tears my heart in two
As I only have one heart
And it belongs to you
And when you came into my life
The sun was shining, sky so blue
I only want to be your wife
And just belong to you
But if in your life there is another
Who means something to you
I don't mean sister or a brother
But I'll always be true to you

So we must have a heart to heart
And talk the whole thing through
And if it means we have to part
I'll always think of you.

Mary Dixon, Meathop, Cumbria

ONE DAY

Wake my darling, open your eyes
Today is bright, full of surprise.
Wake my sweet, stretch out wide
It will be another day I'm full of pride

Play my precious, go explore
There'll be adventures, for you, galore
Play my beau, please envision
Anything you wish, it's your decision

Laugh my poppet, show your glee
Your giggle is a true delight to me
Laugh my gem, express your joy
Your smile is gorgeous, like you my boy.

Hush my love, be still your woe
Daddy's here, I'll never go
Hush my angel, please don't cry
Mummy's here, my love won't die.

Clare Bell, Maryport, Cumbria

MY ENDLESS LOVE

What more can I say?
What else can I do?
To show how much
I do love you

You are my day
My night time too
Our love will last
Our whole life through

The things we share
The moments spent
With you just make
My heart content

My feelings for you
Have no end
A life together
We will spend

Ann Christine Robertson, Workington, Cumbria

ACHIEVING GOLD

Fifty golden years today, ups and downs along the way,
Patience, kindness, love and trust, these ingredients are a must,
Tolerance and loyalty, teamwork and equality,
Mutual generosity, thoughtfulness and honesty,
Building up a life together, promises that last forever,
Sharing laughter, drying tears, growing stronger through the years,
Discussing plans, communication, caring, comfort, dedication,
Special times to bring you pleasure, creating memories to treasure.
Raising a family of you own, proudly watching as it's grown,
Along life's journey, always there, always showing how much you care,
You're a shining example, a double act, kindred spirits, that's a fact.
Fifty years as man and wife, gold medalists in married life.

Kathleen Evans, Wigton, Cumbria

EMOTIONS

I look at you every single day,
The reaction on your face.
The moods I read with expert skill,
To what around takes place.

Do you know what goes on in my mind?
Because you never ask.
Yet would I want you to know?
What goes on behind my mask?

To know a person is so immense
To love and keep their time.
One thing my darling is the fact,
That you will always be mine.

There is however the age old thing,
The mystery is inbound.
The one thing, however much I moan,
My life around you is wound.

Dawn Graham, Barrow-in-Furness, Cumbria

GROWING LOVE

The greatest pleasure is not always love,
Love can be too intense,
A tightrope walked precariously
Between the abyss of jealously
And the hard cliffs of domineering power.

Most people love, and then in time
The poor ones find love drifts,
So one day they look up to see
A stranger where their lover was
And emptiness of feeling takes their place.

The lucky ones are those who find that love
Might seem to have faded, but
It has become distilled, refined
Into a shared experience
In which each is contented just to be

Affectionately yours.

Geoff Hunter, Cockermouth, Cumbria

ONE HUNDRED AND FIFTY DAYS

Do you sit alone
Day after day?
What do you do?
What do you say?
What do you feel
Night after night?
Do you lie awake
And stare at the light?
Are there bars on your window?
Can you still see the sky?
Can you still see the ground?
Or is your window too high?
When you look out at night
Can you still see the moon?
Be strong, just hold on.
You'll be coming home soon.

Tracey Turner, Barrow-in-Furness, Cumbria

BALLAD OF THE WRECKER

Tonight I'm taking my schooner
One last time I'll feel the sea wind
The salt on my lips.
Captain I was, wrecker I am.

Don't wait for me or watch as I sail
And don't think too harshly one that I loved
For youth's reckless tides did sweep me away
But now I know what it is I must do.

This Key West wrecker's gone out to sea
Wheel in my hands, devil behind me
This last wreck's my own, no epitaph
No pirate life, just a grave to make out of reef.

I know what they'll say and it'll be true
But think of me the way I once was -
Damp souwester, carefree smile
No gallows for me, I'll go with my ship.

Don't watch, my love, and don't cry a tear
Just look to the sea and there I'll be -
My boat on the waves, a ghost on the deck
The ghost of a wrecker calling to you.

Ruth Cooper, Bolton, Greater Manchester

YOU PASS ME BY

Though many times you've passed me by,
My heart will never say goodbye.
Affection for you grows and grows,
And makes me yours, though no-one knows
How much I long to hold you near,
As I dream on will you appear.
Within my heart your love is mine,
I draw on it like vintage wine.
The warmth I feel brings forth a sigh,
As I look on you pass me by.

May Foreman, Ashton-under-Lyne, Greater Manchester

LIVING WITH DISABILITY

You shed no tears and your eyes won't tire
You stare into truth and your tongue is knotted tight
You reveal no excuse and you feel no guilt
Your conscience is empty and your body won't burn shame

You are recognised with neglect and your will won't weaken
Your pride extends its strength and you've no desire to
submit
You survive on your nostalgia and resist the unpredictable
beckons from unfamiliar faces.
You seek your ambitions alone without ignorance and your
paces are sturdy
Your visions are genuine and you expect no pity
Your company is your own and your response is negative
Your emotions are trapped and your pressures extinct
Your features are cold and expressions are mysterious and
they fear you

Julie Porter, Eccles, Greater Manchester

RELUCTANT PEN

Mawkishly dated, insincere and limp,
I wouldn't expect it even from a pimp.
The term is totally female in style,
wantonly used and loaded with guile.
Who would be so terribly bland
with an expression penned totally "off-hand?"
Is there feeling or is there not?
Fulsome committal it certainly hasn't got.
Why should one use such a watery mention,
grudgingly easing a little tension?
Does one need to formalise the script
with a lukewarm note barely lipped?
What sort of person could one possibly endear
in conventional terms of yesteryear?
It's just a way of restraining real feeling
that could really get the reader reeling.
Handy phrases taken as a matter of course
must inevitably include, "Affectionately yours"
If the heart can give no more than that,
the way is open to eat one's hat!

John Patterson, Ashton-under-Lyne, Greater Manchester

TIME AFTER TIME

Sing me a song, read me a rhyme
Tell me a story, pour me some wine

Help me remember when life was sublime
Hold me in your arms, in them let me recline

Whisper of love like you used to do
I know you still love me, as I love you

My words no longer needed, no longer mine
Lost for a while, unable to smile

Life is precious we said time after time
No mountain too high for us to climb

Memories are all I have in my silent head
A world of confinement to a single bed

No tears for the past for tears don't last
Just always be mine till the end of my time

Iris Gibson, Ashton-under-Lyne, Greater Manchester

LOVING TIME

Oh, how we love our freedom
Now that summer's here
To stroll down a country lane
Where no two flowers look the same
And peace and happiness reigns

The tall oak trees bend and sway
In a pleasant and gentle breeze
And shade the young children
As they play

The sun shines down upon
The hallowed ground, where once
By a stream we sat, and vowed
Our love would never stray
On the warm and pleasant summer's day

The years have rolled by, but still
We return to our place in the sun
Where once we were young and gay
To again renew the vow we made
On that warm and sunny summer's day.

John Griffin, Davyhulme, Greater Manchester

I'M OKAY I HAVE A FRIEND

Which moments are so precious
in any given day?
The moments are when I'm with you
and we know the world is fine,
because we are together, sharing
thoughts, ideas and time.

Who is the one I rely on
no matter what the cause?
Through laughter, tears until the end
You are, my own true friend.

Marie Kay, Bolton, Greater Manchester

MORNING VISIT

I raked the lawn, the air was raw
Coping with leaves I heard the call
Looking up the sight was thrilling
A perfect vee of wild geese drilling

The leader was a noisy chap
Giving his orders, "Don't leave a gap"
They were flying low this cold morning
Then they were gone, didn't give a warning

The air was still, the silence loud
No blackbird sang in the branches bowed
The gaggle of geese was far away
I raked the leaves thinking what a great day

Dorothy A Harwood, Bolton, Greater Manchester

EMOTIONS RUN HIGH

To love is to bare the soul
Give all that is in your heart
One day you feel like you're cherished
The next like you're pulled apart

Realisation is an electrical charge
Defibrillator hits your chest
It dawns "You love that person"
Fear that you won't stand the test

You are needy and vulnerable at once
But the highs do out weigh the lows
You won't eat you cannot sleep
The stress and strain really shows

You hear their voice on the phone
Reassuring reaffirming their love
Your spirits soar catapulted high
Your heart is like the peace dove

The prize at the end it is worth it
To be at one with your love
You have to be in it to win it
Relax, chill, don't push or shove

Barbara Jardine, Oldham, Greater Manchester

MOTHER LOVE

Things looked bad for little Tim
It looked like he could never win
He was his mother's pride and joy
In fact he was her only boy

Each night she tucked him into bed
His cheerful smile filled her with dread
For he had not got long to live
And needed the love that only she could give

The doctor always did his best
But nature had to do the rest
With little hope of getting right
He had not got a future bright

Mum held his hand to give him hope
A little tear ran down her throat
For money had no value now
So she prayed as only she knew how

That God would welcome little Tim
And he could go and live with him
So mum stayed by and held his hand
While God took him into his promised land

Jim Haslam, Norden, Greater Manchester

SONG FOR MY LANDLORD AT SWANSEA

I'm danged if I know it,
I'm danged if I do,
I'm moithered, dangsarnit,
I'll leave it to you.

Me sheep have got maggots,
Up under their tails,
I'm off to Porthcawl
For a night on the ale.

I've got a new tractor,
I car make it start,
Me combine is buggered,
I car get the parts.

Me cows' got the shits,
They'm all shit up the walls,
The grass goes right through them,
I'm off to Porthcawl.

Me hens are all knackered,
The fox got the geese,
I ay coming back,
You can bugger the lease

Jeremy Greenwood, Bacup, Lancashire

SPRINGTIME AND WINTER

Looking through my window
All sorts are going on
New shoots budding on the trees
Daffodils swaying in the breeze
Ducks are flying, quacking and mating
Blossoms and heather's in bloom
Chasing away the cold and dark of the winters gloom
But oh, I should not talk too soon
For it has now started to snow
Looks just like winter and springtime are making a beauti-
ful show.

Mabel Harrison, Blackburn, Lancashire

REMEMBER ME

Remember me, when I am gone
When memories past still linger on
Remember me on a sunny day
When Nature's kind in every way
Remember me in springtime
When blossoms wreath the trees
And all the flowers in fancy dress
Drift by on a gentle breeze

But to be remembered by those I've loved
Is all that I would ask

'Tis then I ask, remember me.

Marion Kaye, Poulton-le-Fylde, Lancashire

PASSED

An angel to me,
You guide my life.
A secret power,
You are my light.

The first and last thing,
I see each day,
My dreams, fantasies,
I have with me.

Waking to feel you,
By my side.
Intense emotions,
I open my eyes.

Your spirit and soul,
Will always be close.
Having the memories,
Meaning the most.

Suzanne Jenkinson, Preston, Lancashire

HIM AND ME

In the days when passion ran hot.
And the blood sang in my veins.
Our union was ecstatic and sweet,
We were replete.

Passion and the blood cool down.
A slower sweetness now combines.
Where love and closeness have become,
A gentler loving time.

Gillian Sawyer, Morecambe, Lancashire

THE ROSE

I've heard love's a rose,
They say it's beauty immaculate.
It blooms after winter snow
And gives us joy forever more.

But I've heard there's thorns
They're made of a sorrowful past
that creeps up for years before,
And so the heart is quickly torn.

But hidden far away,
Quite near if you try,
You'll see the one that's brave,
That doesn't an easy way crave.

Before the others it arose
And stayed all the while.
And when the thorns have cleared, I see,
You are my love, my only rose.

Harriet Pomfret, Clitheroe, Lancashire

GIGANTIC

Like a giant snowball you preside
Over the snow flurries falling
To this freezing earth

You stay calm in this confusion
Unfolding below you
You roll out to watch
Over this freezing earth

It is below freezing
Is this pleasing you?
Are you glad to be cool?

Am I the fool who you rule?
Is this pleasing?
I'm just teasing

Please stay
For the next millennium

Margery Mahon, Preston, Lancashire

THE LOTTERY OF TRUE MINDS AND MONOTONY

Take the milkman for example
He has another man's woman
He surprises her with roses and full cream gold top
She likes to dress up until the pain fades
When it does she eats poison chocolates until the bleeding
stops
Even at the height of our notoriety we were far more
anonymous than she
Only the music kept us alive while the pain insisted into us
At night
Deserting the common bank
We deceived ourselves with metre and syntax and stories
from the ministry
Where original thoughts flopped into a pool of tightly knit-
ted mischief like lazy frogs in summer time
Our eccentricity hummed encouragement to past lovers
Who infected our heartbeat to monitor their loss
It was a lot of fun
But you needed tears and time to think and darkness to
sing to.

Tony Cullen, Coppull, Lancashire

A YOUNG MAN'S LAMENT

Four grey walls
and a heavy door,
I wonder if he can
take any more?

He asked a priest to
show him God's ways,
but his shame and guilt
stayed with him all
his days.

A crumpled note lay
by his bed,
"I love you Mom,"
the note read.

Today I will be as
free as a bird,
so please forgive me Lord,
I mean every word.

Pamela McNamara, Heysham, Lancashire

THE CORRIDORS OF TIME

The corridors of time I feel
Have answers hidden deep
Unknown to any mortals
Cryptic clues within our sleep
Paths erased and gateways locked
Though keys exist its true
But only minds with inner eyes
Can step beyond and through

James Michael Thomas, Preston, Lancashire

YOUR SMILE

I made your smile your epitaph,
You left your smile behind.
I see your smile, I hear your laugh,
The sweetness of your mind.

Your children knew your happy smile,
Your friends remember too,
That every day along the way
Your gentleness shone through.

We spoke of smiles, believed in them,
Smiles carried through each day,
You taught us all to smile and laugh,
We treasure this today.

You leave behind this epitaph
Of happiness to share.
We think of you, your lovely smile,
And know you know we care.

Helen Melrose, Blackpool, Lancashire

OUR ENGLAND

Do people ever stop to think
How lucky that they are
Living in this country
Which excels most things by far
No hurricanes, tornadoes
No drought or real floods
Folk may moan at the climate
But truthfully it is good
There is no greater land elsewhere
Than England in the spring
The summers are not enough
And autumn has a sting
The winters are not bad at all
Compared with other lands
We've all the water that we need
And lots of food on hand
So just give all these things a thought
Every now and then
And thank the Lord that you were born
A lucky Englishman

Carmel Allison, Blackpool, Lancashire

RESIGNEDLY YOUR VALENTINE

Your tidy gift
of ideal love or friendship or both
came flouncing through the door
to a plethora of uproar.
Vermillion petals pursed out at me
kissing the fragrant air.
How it adorned the place:
Flushing scarlet plushes to my face.
To everyone else it was harmless;
Its dumb-brained blank stare.
What a disgrace you are.
What a humiliation.
Emotionally stunted to stale roses:
sucking at their airbrushed callow folds.
What impresses a girl is understanding,
careful listening.
There we were, one and the other,
red-cheeked.
It with a fake show of budding love
and I with a withering, cringing pain.

Wendy Woodhead, Blackpool, Lancashire

THE BARONESS AMOS

I met a lovely lady
She spoke of lands afar
Where people died from lack of food
Their colour was a bar

She asked us to help the refugees
The asylum seekers too
Whatever their race or creed
To see what we could do

All the national charities
Were pledged to give their aid
To change the hearts of leaders
To tell them we were bade

I think of little children
The old, the sick, the maimed
We'll do our best to help them
We'll stand up and be named

We think of Martin Luther King
Mandela and such men
They stood for freedom and for liberty
We'll take up arms and pen

Jean Turner, Preston, Lancashire

FOND MEMORIES

Reflections
In still waters
Recall those
First enchanted
Embraces.
Days when
You to me
I to you
Vowed love
Eternally.

Reflections
In still waters
Whisper thanks
For all you gave.
But though my
Fond heart recalls
Your every vow,
My head asks:
"Where are
You now?"

John A Rickard, Wallasey, Merseyside

UNCOMPLETE

My heart quickens with anticipation
I know that you are near
I feel your presence ever closer and my heart aches
Just for you to hold me in your arms for all time
Many an hour I missed you
Many a moment I wondered
Had I dreamt you into my life
You are my soul mate, my missing piece
Without you I am incomplete
Ever aching, ever dreaming, ever needing
Hold me, need me, love me, complete me.

Vikki Payne, St Helens, Merseyside

THE FLAME IN MY HEART

A certain look
A certain touch
A warm, full smile
That says so much

I know you by heart
And all the things that you do
Your patience and love
Always helps to see me through

You can brighten the day with
A romantic glance
You make the flame in my heart
Flicker and dance

George Donnellan, Wallasey, Merseyside

REMEMBER

Remember smiling eyes, sunburned cheeks
Love-filled knowing looks, no need to speak,
Remember walking through a woodland glade,
Gazing in wonder at flowers of every shade.

Do not be sad when I am far away,
It was my time to go, I could no longer stay.

My life with you was special, one I'll truly miss,
So, my own beloved I blow one last sweet kiss.

Though memories of me may fade
As time goes by,
Remember me with love
Then say goodbye.

Lil Bordessa, Liverpool, Merseyside

BRITISH GRIT

Love is a thing we can never live without
Sharing ones sorrows, ones joy this is life no doubt
Health, happiness and loving is our strongest desire
And the simplest things in life there is no future
It's farewell to our very own British culture.

But why sit back and just watch it die
Get off your backside and don't eat humble pie
Go forth and take up the challenge of life
The pioneer spirit in the days of yore is now rife.

It's idle hands that are controlled by the devil
For true British grit there is no need for evil
Get rid of the deadwood, make way for the new
Don't hang around, join in and become one of the crew
So with loving care and gentle tenderness
I say good luck, good night and God bless.

William Reilly, Liverpool, Merseyside

THE RELUCTANT GUEST

Can poetry appear upon request?
Only, I fear, sullenly and ill-dressed;
No colour, scent or liveliness of feature,
Simply a commonplace and careless creature.
But if the moment's right and of her choice
One feels the presence, hears the authentic voice
Then opens up the soul to blend with hers
In hopeful cadences of harmonious verse.

I'm trying now to coax her into being,
She gazes back, eyes bright but still unseeing.
She's well aware, the wicked one, that she
Holds all the aces, and with hidden glee
Awaits her moment of divine release
To grant me beauty and an inner peace.
But ah, as you can see, poor stuff till then
Emerges with reluctance from this pen.
Forgive the stumbling effort that I send,
I'm simply at the mercy of my friend.

Josephine Offord, Southport, Merseyside